EN ROUTE TO D DAY

TWICE DEAD PLUCKED UP BY THE ROOTS

Rev. Dw Paige

PUBLISH
AMERICA

PublishAmerica
Baltimore

ISBN: 1-60813-851-8
PUBLISHED BY PUBLISHAMERICA, LLLP
www.publishamerica.com
Baltimore

Printed in the United States of America

Note that all names of individuals and places have been changed to protect the privacy of those individuals and places.

The highest spirit of dedication, and demonstration of deepest Love, I hereby dedicate this Labor of Love and Patience of Hope to my honored Life's Companion, Julia Ann Paige. In the same spirit of heavenly cooperation, which they, my Friends, have shown; I, likewise dedicate this work to them, Rev. Dr. John William Wacker, with his faithful, Covenant wife, Mrs. Mable Jerline Wacker. Truly, with us, they have been through fire and through water; and we certainly count them included as Ministry Partners with Us.

Rev. and Mrs. William Paige

This book reveals how human beings can be here on Earth.

Jesus is Real Faith is real walk hand in hand every day with Jesus
Faith will always win.

ACKNOWLEDGEMENT

First let me say, that this book is not about me as a private individual, as such, for my life history is not now, nor has it ever been, in the past, in any way appealing, influential, attractive, or desirous in any manner. The only reason any detail is given in reference to my life prior to acceptance of Jesus, is to give readers a glimpse of where I have come from, without God, to where I have come to with Jesus as my Lord and Savior, and which will ultimately tell the story of a FAITH COVENANT RELATIONSHIP with our LORD and SAVIOR JESUS CHRIST.

Many Biblical references are mentioned within the text of this writing, but perhaps more than any other, Matthew 6:33, Psalms 91, and Daniel 4:35 helped to establish a operable mindset for this FAITH COVENANT RELATIONSHIP. And the enabling power of The Holy Spirit provided me the strength to forge ahead, when seemingly we were in direct contradiction to everyone, and everything we knew. The quote of John Johnson's mentor; "if it's of man it's bad, if it's of the devil it's wicked, but if it's of God, it just plain doesn't make any sense," proved to be more then true. As we continued to play this thing to the end, many unwitting, caring, and non-caring individuals, Christian, and non Christian were seemingly moved within the sphere of God's providence to do as He had purposed (with or without their consent), to bring me to the final conclusion of this faith walk in triumph over Satan and every Demonic influence that attempted to thwart my faith and belief in God, and what he had told me through prophesies, and divine revelation.

Let me state emphatically, I believe in, 3 John vs. 2. In fact one cannot read HOLY WRIT without coming to that very viable and vivid truth. Albeit there are many places within God's Word, most notably the book of JOB, which describes critical, and severe testing, and proving times. I well remember Dr. Roth precious remarks; "I don't know what it takes to satisfy the demands of a righteous God." The very sound of this truth seems to stem from some very critical testing within his life probably in reference to formation of our beloved ATB. But despite all of the credible evidence within HOLY WRIT for this type thing, one is quickly characterized, and labeled irrational, or worse yet a loony toon, or el crazo, by those within the church who relate to a materialistic mindset. They seemed to think that for one to walk by faith is outdated and non relevant to the WILL OF GOD, in the modernistic age of which we live. Ironically, the local church of which I was called to serve as assistant pastor was no exception.

It seemed to be the testing ground for this faith walk, which was similar in nature to that of one of our friends, God put with us. At the height of his test, he and his wife were put right in the midst of several affluent, prominent, wealthy, and prosperous, parishioners with means to do as they pleased, of whom they ministered to routinely, (because of a pastor who was too busy with his self employment), but despite the continued critical, and necessary ministry, and with needs (personal and ministerial) readily apparent, neither the (God professing) parishioners, nor the pastor, (for which he was receiving a pastor's salary), did not bother to lift a finger in support. Many chilling stories were told reflecting on the impassive, unsympathetic, and unresponsive attitude these individuals had in reference to the church needs, or to our friend who was working as a associate pastor, by faith, supposedly because the church couldn't afford to pay more than one full time pastor.

The overall general consensus of the public, and church parishioners, alike within this area, believe (reference ministers) that ministry is not a job, but a pleasurable pastime during off work hours. A factor I feel that contributes to this belief is that better then three fourth of the clergy within this general area hold full time jobs, (perhaps for the love of money, greed, or materialism), and minister part time even though they receive adequate salaries to sustain themselves, from the church they pastor.

The overriding command I had received from God, for this faith walk was fulltime ministry, no secular employment. For the record I was not keen on the idea of going back into the secular employment market, having left to be involved with ministry fulltime, but I would have gladly done so many times over, rather than to endure the stigma and the mounting pressures associated with this walk. But despite all Hell being against us, the wife and I continued our walk only by and through the ENABLING POWER OF THE HOLY SPIRIT.

One might call this supposition, but somehow I feel that many churches, ministers, and parishioners alike are being tested for their faithfulness, (as to their means, in time, and finances) in the ongoing proclamation of the Gospel of Christ. It could very well be a determinate factor as to their continued ability in that proclamation. Luke 12:48

In the ever widening circle of financial disaster throughout our beloved nation, and around the world, perhaps in accordance with

Proverbs 13:22, & Ecclesiastes 2:26, and, if the many prophetic preachers are right, the vast riches of our land, will be redistributed to those who have been found faithful in proclamation of the Gospel of Christ.

Again I call to attention Roth's remarks; "I would hate to stand before my God knowing that I didn't do all to explore and to bring into being every available media of ministry possible."

It's not what Christ can do for us, but what can we do for Christ. For we can be well assured that when we do everything we know to do for Christ, He in turn will do everything for us. John 12:32

When one comes into a proper relationship with our Lord, we will not need to be reminded of our commitment for it will literally burn within our hearts to follow Him, in every possible way.

CHILDHOOD BACKGROUND

I was reared in a God Fearing home, with a devout mother, who chose to rear me by herself. Church teachings, she felt, prohibited her from remarriage, consequently forcing her to live by herself. She entrusted my care while working to a providentially placed couple that treated me as a very special grandbaby. With only one daughter, alienated from them, they treated me with a special grandparent love. They along with my mother reared me in the best manner possible, giving me all of the Christian love, and teachings possible. At the time of high school, my mother pressed me hard to enroll in a parochial school for which I wanted no part. However in those days parents carried the authority, and not the children.

HIGH SCHOOL YEARS

So off I went to a combination Christian high school, and college in the same city, I lived. The school had dedicated staff to insure proper training and counseling, reference one's future. With reluctance, I attended all four years of the Christian high school. Each day during the school year, we were required to sit through anointed chapel services. One cannot be around a place of this nature, for any length of time, without coming to the knowledge of Jesus. Just as His word says: Isaiah 55:11

So for the balance of my high school years, I not only lived and learned to respect God, and His Word, but come to know Him as my own personal Savior. The spirit was willing, but I still had my own plans. Part of the time I walked in obedience to God, other times I went my own way. Near the end of my junior year, I begin to feel a tug on my conscience to be in ministry. I discussed the possibility with my mother, but she had no formal training in this field and promptly dismissed the idea. I was very reluctant, and timid about discussing

Christ with any one, so I chose to go my own way. After all this was the furthest thing from my mind. I wanted a career with excitement, pomp, riches, popularity, a family, a home, and I wanted to take care of my mother, the way she had taken care of me. I wanted nothing to do with preaching. Without casting blame on anyone I do feel that if I would have received proper counseling, reference ministry, I possibly would have reconsidered. I was surrounded with good Godly men and women who would have done everything within their power to help me receive the proper schooling, but I chose to ignore the call of God. My Godparents no doubt would have funded my entire ministry school, for they routinely prayed for me to be a minister, but I did not heed, to the call of God.

POST HIGH SCHOOL YEARS AND CAREER WITHOUT GOD

After my high school graduation in 62, I chose to enter into a secular job, with no fulfillment. I started jumping from job to job. The name of the game for me was making money and having a new car. Having received earlier training from The Boy Scouts and their motto of always "BEING PREPARED," I always tried to live up to that motto. Likewise, I realized the importance of education, but never attended a college per se. Albeit I took various courses to qualify me for licensing, as an Auctioneer, Real Estate Broker, (sales, management, appraising), Plumbing contractor, Car Dealer, gun dealer, and notary etc. We had a complete liquidation business. I had enough licenses to paper a wall with, but really could have cared less about any of them. From about (1965 –1979), I worked fulltime as an insurance inspector normal work hours, and then would run my self—employment after that. Talk about diversification, I had it all, but what good was it. I had no fulfillment or pride in my work, it was just a job.

As I looked back on my life now, I feel God gave me many windows of opportunities to preach, especially in the earlier years after graduation, as the wife and I had many meaningful times with the Lord. But I ignored the constant nagging within my heart to preach especially, when I would grow close to God, but I continued to follow the same path as before, not really surrendering my life to the Will of God.

MARRIAGE—DIVORCE

Well God let me have my own way. God will never force His will on any one. But was I, in for a surprise. Following nine years of marriage, and two adorable children the first tragedy occurred. I lost my family, to divorce. My finances spiraled downward to less than fifty percent of my once prized financial goals, and reputation, for which I often boasted. My once promising career seemed to take on an ominous turn for the worse. I lost my will to work or live, I just existed. I searched for answers but there seemed to be none.

The radio evangelist described it well: "Having been married and then divorced was like two potatoes cooked in a pot, mashed and then being separated. You were no longer two individuals but two fragmented individuals." No better way to put it, and no truer words were ever spoken.

For the better part of two years, I wondered aimlessly to and fro, traveling thousands of miles searching for something; anything that would fill the void in my life caused by the divorce. Nothing seemed to satisfy. The pastor of our church counseled me many times, but still yet I had my own thoughts and my own will. Determined to do as I pleased, God let me do just that.

With the frame of mind one is in, following a divorce one cannot be efficient at anything he does. My career seemingly came to a standstill. I began to search for something; I didn't know what, just something that would pop for me, but to no avail.

Let me tell you, when one can pick up a newspaper the size of the Chicago Tribune, or the Indianapolis Star, and find nothing in the employment ads, that suits your fancy, you are in bad trouble.

Well everything that I opted not to go into the ministry for, a career with excitement, pomp, riches, and popularity, family, a home, etc. vanished before my very eyes. Luke 17:33, Mark 8:35

By now my interest in Christianity begin to fade. I rarely attended church, blaming God, for my marriage problems, not to mention all of the other ensuing difficulties, I was encountering. I begin to patronize the bars and nightclubs regularly, not really because they appealed to me, but it seemed to be a place where all the loners hung out. When one goes through a divorce your social life is all but stopped, forcing you to take on new acquaintance, sometimes good, and sometimes bad. Many well meaning, well intentioned individuals are forever scarred mentally, and or physically, because of such relationships. This would be a good out reach for a Bible believing Church to get involved with. The best time to reach one is when they are reeling from such circumstances.

NEW MARRIAGE

In 1976 the Lord divinely orchestrated a caring young lady in my life, with two children, with a passion to serve Christ. But for the most part, I gave Christ no heed, attending church only when I felt like it. When finding out about my sparse attendance, she insisted on going with me. Well that seemed to pick me up, and give me the drive that I once had, at least temporarily. The people at church fell in love with my wife to be, and her two children. The church reached out to the both of us. That lasted for a good while, even after we were married, in (April 77). By this time the wife was really getting involved with church activity. She seemed to be there every time the door was open. I was almost jealous of her continued interest in the seemingly never ending church activity.

HIS AND HERS KID PROBLEMS

Shortly after our marriage, (his) and (her) kid problems begin to surface. There seemed to be no solution. If both of us would have had a deep personal relationship with Christ, we could have overcome. But that was far from the truth. We had a form of Godliness but no power. And when I say that I don't diminish my wife's sincere desire to serve God, for she tried to serve God in the best possible manner she could under the conditions.

Her jealousy over my children, and my relationship with them, including what I did for them, (I had an insatiable desire to do for my children more than ever since the divorce), caused much anger, resentment, and dissention, between us, and towards the children. With no peace in the home while my children were present, I felt indisposed to bring them to my house. Likewise I made life miserable for her two children, in return. Neither one of us had any time for the other's children.

Mentioning this to some individuals in the same circumstance, they stated; "You think it's bad when you have (his), and (her) children, wait till you have (his), (her), and (our) children." Well there is a lot of truth to that statement.

Statistics indicate that more than seventy-five percent of all second marriages end in divorce, over children by the previous marriage.

For the record, let me tell you plain and simple, the only thing that will resolve this wide spread problem the world over, is the LOVE OF JESUS CHRIST in one's heart.

Many beautiful and adoring children are forever scarred in the relentless search for equality within mixed marriages, and will continue even unto the next generation, without God's love. In God's eyes there is no (his) and (her) children but (our) children.

Neither one of us knew how to deal with this tragic problem consequently; we ended up splitting 15 times in the first 7 years of our marriage. (See our book on (His) and (Her) Kids) Our relationship (of our own making) was pure hell.

By every account, we should have been divorced; in fact papers were filed towards the end, but were never followed through with, and we continued on, knowing the pain we faced again in a world by our self. We had already been there and done that.

Relatives played a big part in the unrest of these troubled times as well as the church. In fact, the church seemed to take sides in the kid problems seeing only one side, consequently alienating me. In short they had never walked in our shoes, and really didn't understand anything of the problem. Since being involved with ministry I have always tried to make it a point not to be one sided in my counseling but to include both. Somehow God miraculously held us together, the wife and I believe for this time.

I JUST DIDN'T CARE ANY LONGER

By the late (80's) I was of the mind set I didn't care anymore. Let me tell you that was, a dangerous place to be. I had become what my wife, and mother described as Devil possessed. I begin doing things that I never dreamed I would, or could be involved with, but apart from God, man has the propensity to commit the most horrible, and horrendous deeds.

GOD BEGINS TO MOVE

My praying mother and wife, who had by now begun to be more deeply involved with God, begin to seek God on my behalf. They both continued to reach out to me, not preaching, or scolding, but loving me, and forgiving me. The thing that really began to break the ice was the Christian songs (the old time Hymns) that my wife would continually play for her own encouragement, as well as mine. I was not easy to live with. I was going through a very troubling period of time, and I made every one aware of it. I didn't find out until this book was being written that my mother had encouraged my wife to stand on 1 Corinthians 10:13. Well that is true in every walk we make while living for God. He always will provide a way when there seems to be no way.

A BRAIN DEAD COUCH POTATO REVIVED

2 Corinthians 5:17, and John 10:10

While I was far from God, I still had reverence for Him. But seemingly I was unable for many years now to have any meaningful relationship with Him. There were just too many problems in my life. By saying this I don't mean to diminish God's power, but the Bible does speak, in John 6:44, John 6:65 reference this.

By the same token I think just being in the same room with all of the Christian music, God's Marvelous Light Shown through as mention in 1 Peter 2:9.

This allowed me to see my ram shackled, crumbling, and Godless life style. I had become a brain dead, TV couch potato, (drug enhanced). I began to crave for knowledge about our beginning, about the hereafter, about life in general, a craving that I had never experience before.

If you recall in the late (80's early 90's) Israel and the mid east began to take on new meaning to the world. That in and of itself, sparked interest in me, for I was well aware of God's promise reference Israel. And I well remember the miraculous intervention that occurred during the (67) War.

Thank God for the faithfulness of men like Dr. Ray Jamison, and Dr. Jim Anderson who continually brought us updates Via TV, of happenings in Israel, as it related to prophecy!

Beyond the Christian music my wife was playing, this was the only other ministry outlet I had. I had not attended church for several years, reason here before mentioned. But now all of a sudden, church seemed to be something I desired.

I had a friend Rev. Lotus within the church that was willing to go the extra mile with me, despite the previous difficulties; and I had all the confidence in him one could have. Having heard the prophecy messages from the Rev. Jamison and Rev. Anderson I, scheduled some meetings with him to discuss what I was hearing. Did it mean what I thought it did? Was Christ ready to come back? My mind went wild with all types of questions. The Holy Spirit was bringing to remembrance the things that I had learned when I was a part of the Body of Christ.

Somehow God, in His Divine Wisdom, was drawing me into a relationship with Him, of which I had fallen far away. Some say you can't lose your Salvation, but had I died, in this current state, I would have been lost, despite my Christian heritage.

Shortly thereafter, I went to the church I grew up in, to hear a former pastor, Dr. Steven Pearl preach. I never will forget the sermon, for it struck home to me just as the Holy Spirit intended.

The sermon he preached was drifting beyond the Call of God.

The story he told was of a little boy who decided to go on a picnic with his kitten. Having arrived at the river's edge, he begin to snack, and romp with the kitten. Three drunks from up the river, seeing the fun the boy was having, decided to wrest the kitten out of the little boy hands and take it up the river. When returning to their camp site they then threw the kitten into the fast moving water. The kitten drifted helplessly downstream but heard its master's voice calling its name out, "come back, come back," the kitten responded by working its way towards the edge of the river bank, allowing it's master to rescue it from the frigid waters. The second time the drunks did the same thing over again, this time they threw the kitten further out into the waters. Again its master called out as before, likewise the kitten responded, allowing its master to rescue it. The third time, seeing what had happened, the drunks took control of the kitten again, but this time they threw it far out into the river. Again, as it was being swept down the river, its master frantically called out to it, but this time it was beyond its master's voice. The kitten was lost without any hope of being rescued. The pastor likened

21

the story to that of an individual who time after time had been called by Christ, but failed to respond; consequently drifting beyond the call of God.

Wow! Did that hit me! And the Holy Spirit was quick to remind me, of my Christian Heritage, and the Christian circle of friends I had, and what a shame, it would be, if I were to be lost.

THE STRAW THAT BROKE THE CAMEL'S BACK.

The final straw that broke the camel's back was our financial condition. My once promising career had plummeted, and spiraled out of control, causing financial chaos. I had lost my desire, to even be involved with the business world, much less continue working in it. There seemed to be no simple solution. I was in debt far above any equitable solution. I had come through many financial storms in my life, especially after divorce, but now everything I owned, was about to be lost. There seemed to be a higher power, if you will, at work, although I didn't realize it at the time. In this same period of time, the wife had gone to the grocery store one day, and when returning home, she indicated that there was a foreclosure notice posted on the store window, reference our real estate. The meaning of this was not good. Fortunately, I was able to avert a foreclosure by seeking council. By now, I knew I was at my end. As I lay there that day pondering what to do, the Holy Spirit was quick to draw me into His Presence.

REPENTANCE TIME

I said; "Lord I don't want to come to you just because of all this trouble." But for some reason I couldn't resist asking Him to come into my life. Up until this time I had not had a desire to serve God for years. Yes, I thought about it, but the desire, the driving force if you will, was just not there. As stated earlier, in accordance with Holy Writ, I believe a person has to be called, into Salvation.

Many prayers such as above had been prayed over the years, by me, but for some reason I was never able to have a meaningful relationship with Christ. But that day it was different. The desire was gone to do wrong, and I had a desire to do right. From that day on, I begin to have a relationship with the master. I wandered many times far, from the straight and narrow, but somehow he chose to keep His hands on me, and kept the desire to do right in my heart. The songs the wife played, the sermons on ATB by The Elite of God's Elect, my mother's prayers, my wife's prayer, had all served their purpose. I had been born again. I begin to grow in the Lord, becoming so happy at times, that I couldn't contain. This was in the year perhaps (91).

BANKRUPTCY AND A NEW BEGINNING

Our financial problems did not abate. Many agonizing days were spent pondering just what road to take. Reorganization was out of the question. One banking friend advised that the lending community would think none the less of me, one way or the other. With every alternate seemingly closed we filed bankruptcy. That was not my will but seemingly, I had little else I could do. Having been involved with the business world, as I had, I knew where this road would lead, and the many problems, it would cause. But the Lord, too, had his hands on the entire proceedings.

Everything I had represented in my business career with or without Christ was good credit. The motto that I referred earlier too, was always on my mind day and night. Be prepared. I couldn't stand a dead beat person who just floated with the tide "come what may" with no desire to do better. Yet, I had become dangerously close to that same thing, but I believe God had his all enabling hand on me even through those times.

A BUSINESS TO RUN

Now I still had a business to run, but it was as if one hand was tied behind my back. In my auctions, we always used banking personnel to clerk, now they shied away from me. The credit that I had found so easy earlier had all but vanished and it seemed as though the walls came tumbling down.

But somehow after accepting Christ something new was beginning to happen. My auction sales begin to pick up and we received several large sales, keeping me busy fulltime at having auctions.

The next boost came in my car lot. We specialized in selling older vehicles. Strangely enough, no other car lot could sell such cars, which put me in a market by myself. We switched our operation to a buy here pay here lot, giving us the lead in our area for this type sale. Surprising one could even sell this type vehicle, but we were able to keep going fulltime in the business.

In addition my rental business spontaneously exploded.

Now more than ever, The Lord begin to magnify His self to me in greater proportions, then I had ever known. I had never really come to depend much on God. This was an attribute of my mother, but it seemed off base to me. She had little or no interest to do anything but work in a factory. Certainly not my desire, nor will.

Yet at the same time, I observed my mother acquiring a house for which she had prayed for many years and the Lord worked it out. She always wanted a house with yellow siding, and lo and behold following her retirement a government program came in, and spruced her house up with new windows, and updated electrical service, and you guessed it, yellow vinyl siding. What a great place to live, in the Shadows of the Almighty.

Even though my business was sparking, I still needed credit, but do to the bankruptcy I was unable to obtain any.

A NEW HOUSE

Surprisingly God always made a way. Many: times in unbelievable incidents. And that was the case with another house, He helped me to acquire, following my bankruptcy. Three years prior, to bankruptcy we had made an offer on this given house in the amount of ($17,000.00). But before the offer could be presented to the owner, someone else offered to pay the listed price, of ($24,000.00), consequently the broker opted not to let my offer be made.

We had out grown the house we lived and reared our family in. We had turned it into three apartments, living in one, using one for our office, and the wife's beauty shop, and renting one. We had no room to sdd on to, our own quarters causing us to be cramped. However our income never seemed to enable us to live in a single house.

Now 3 years later the contract owner of the same house that I earlier had made an offer on, (who I knew well) called me, indicating that he was having trouble with the contract buyer who had purchased the house. They were running delinquent on their payments.

He wanted me to contact them to see what their intentions were, reference keeping the house. In response to his request, I made the contact, for which they assured me everything was kosher. I informed the owner, of their favorable intentions. Approximately one month later the owner called again, and said they had vacated the house, and wanted me to secure it.

During the ensuing conversation he reminded me of my earlier offer made 3 years prior, and wanted to know if I was still interested. I said: "yes, but not at the price they had paid." I further stated I would have to list it, before buying it. He asked; "why?" and I told him it would enable me to receive a brokers fee, which in turn could be applied towards the down payment. He then asked; "how much I would be willing to pay," and I responded, ($15,000.00). He then asked; what the selling commission would cost and I told him ($900.00). He in return said; "why don't you just give me ($500.00) down and buy it." I don't need to remind you I didn't waist anytime getting that contract signed the same day, even though I had to drive 140miles.

When I first purchased the house I had intentions of renting it out, as I didn't feel I could afford both rent, and utilities. Likewise we had little furniture living only in a three room apt. Well that night neither one of us could sleep for we both wanted to live in that house even though we didn't feel we could afford it. But the Lord had different plans, and when we awoke He begin to let his plans be known. We decided that we would move into the house and rent the apt out we was living in.

And so the first thing Monday morning we begin to have utilities turned on and we moved in.

At about the same time, I listed several large auction sales, and in addition, our car sales exploded further, enabling me to furnish the house completely, with new furnishings.

AN OVERWHELMING DESIRE
TO JUST DO SOMETHING FOR GOD

This all occurred the week of our annual camp meeting. I don't mind to tell you the wife, and I, both were bubbling over with the Joy of the Lord. The wife and I attended camp meeting all week, hardly able to contain. I had an over whelming desire, or craving from within to do something great for the Lord. I didn't know what I just wanted to do something. As stated earlier, I was reared around this Holiness Camp sight, and knew many people. The house that we had just bought was located across the street from the camp ground, and parochial school, that I had attended, and was once owned by a former General Superintendent Of the church.

While talking to a friend before church one night Joe Carpenter I was telling him about the miraculous events surrounding the purchase of the house. I told of my desire to just do something, for God, to repay Him for His kindness. He then told me of his recent mission trips to Africa, and the blessings he had received from it. Like me he could hardly contain his joy as he told me of the many details of the trip. He further stated that they were planning another trip to Africa the first of the year (93).

I told him of my desire to go. The price of ($2,000.00), seemed to be beyond my reach. As I told him that, He said "Oh! If it's the Lords will for you to go he will make it possible." Well! That wasn't the first time I had heard that expression. Statements such as this always reminded me of my mother, and her faith. That worried me, for I had never thought of myself as being dependent upon God.

Later he put me in contact with the team leader, and I begin to make planes to go to Africa, without any money. August was half gone and time was ticking away. Again I had no back up credit cards, or any other source from which I could draw money. My business was going good, but would it be that good, to allow me to pay that much cash up front. That didn't seem to be feasible. Proverbs 3:5

26

A MIRACLE TRIP

With the dead line of payment approaching, something unusual happened at the car lot. I rarely stayed at the lot, (for I had a man employed in that capacity), and I had returned home. It came to my attention through a neighbor that an accident had occurred on my car lot. Being friends with the police department, I called and asked what was going on. The radio operator responded that someone had run into the back of my building. My building set on a corner lot readily accessible from the front and side. But the rear of it was separated and protected by a vacant thirty foot lot on the edge of an embankment covered with trees. No access whatever. I said; "You mean they ran into the side of it, don't you." He says; "no, it was hit from the rear." "Impossible" I said, and went to the car lot. Well sure enough just as the officer had stated, a car had ran into the back of my building. This car, it seems, had struck another car at the intersection a whole block to the east, and rear of my lot, causing it to careen out of control, swerving through a vacant lot, dodging six to eight vehicles, through the clump of trees, up the embankment, and into my building. Damage was limited but because of this accident, I was able to take the missions trip. Unbelievable!

Well at the last minute we were forced to change our itineraries from Africa to St. Kitts, West Indies. The Lord seemed to be smiling on me all the time. I shall never forget the day following New Years day (93), that I, boarded the jet, heading for the beautiful Caribbean.

For the first time since my business career began, I was able to spend ten glorious days away from my business, (a business that I had chose apart from God, even at the expense of His call on my life) of which by now had become a real pain. The Lord let me have my own way, consequently causing my nose to be ground into the prison of my own making. Beyond one seven day trip, I had never been away for more than three to four days, and then it caused more problems then what it was worth. Well to make a long story short: It was as my friend had said, a Joy to just serve the Lord in this capacity. My! What, a glorious and blessed time. We assisted in building a new convocation hall, all for the cause of Christ. I knew for the first time what it meant to labor for Christ. Yes I missed the family, but the joy and thrill of this trip was unexplainable. Luke 17:33 Mark 8:35

There are no adequate words to describe God's presence during and after the trip. I felt as though I would explode. Two friends of different churches ask if I would give a talk on my trip. Even though I was an auctioneer, I still was unable to speak with any degree of perfection, so reluctantly I accepted. The first talk was at Johnson Chapel. I had ample study time but did not have any training relative to giving speeches, or sermons, and I was simply scared to death. I used the text Matthew 16:18.

Well something strange came over me that night, as I stood with stammering lips trying to tell of the awesome trip I had been on.

CALLED TO THE MINISTRY

Somehow I knew that night, as I stood behind that Sacred Desk, what I should have done 30 years ago, and by Gods help, what I would do the rest of my life, if possible. There was just something about it, I couldn't explain. That night came and went as one of the highlighted nights of my life. Following that talk, I then went to another church, to give a second talk. Different setting and format but still was just as challenging as before.

I kept feeling more and more pressure upon me to do something, but I didn't know what, but God did.

Next on our schedule was the annual prophecy conference at Tampa Florida. This conference was a must, as it, and its director had impacted our lives so greatly. And again the Lord supplied the money for us to take that trip by air for another week. Psalms 37:4

Well I still didn't know what I wanted to do, but something just laboring for The Lord. For some reason the course, Homiletics kept coming to me. I had earlier discussed this course with a friend when he, for some unknown reason had alluded to it in reference to our conversation. The name seemed to interest me, but I really didn't inquire as to its content. Now I had this nagging feeling about trying to take the Homiletics course. I inquired of some friends, where I might take a college course by correspondence that would be accepted by the higher criticism. They referred me to Indiana Holiness University at Marion, Indiana.

Contacting them they confirmed that they had such a course. Seemingly with an inward compelling force, I ordered it. Once I received it, I begin to make a perusal of it, and consequently a complete study of it. Was it by an inglorious hand that I chose this course, the content of which was (sermon preparation). It seemed to be a medicine to my brain dead, drug induced, TV, couch potato mentality. I mentioned earlier of my craving to learn about life in general, the beginning, the end, and everything between. Now this seemed to satisfy the craving. Unlike the many other courses I had tried to take, but never finished, I couldn't lay it down.

Within three weeks I finished the course, the business ran itself, and strangely enough I made more money during them three weeks then before. What is it? Seek ye first the Kingdom of God. Matthew 6:33 Well I mailed it in, and anxiously awaited the results. Much to my surprise, when receiving the course back I received a (A-) Wow! I was shocked. I told the wife then, if it was that easy to get some college credit under my belt, I was going to do it. So I enrolled in another course. Shortly thereafter, I found out that if I would complete an additional five required courses, that I could obtain a student ministerial license. Wow! I jumped at the chance.

In order to receive a student ministerial license you had to be a member of a local Church within our denomination, and from that point, be recommended by the local church board, to the district board. I had alluded earlier to the problems that I had had within that given church, reference our marital difficulties years ago. Well God's love had invaded my heart, and somehow it didn't seem to matter any longer. So I applied even within the same church, not sure of their reaction, but God had healed their heart as well as mine. Nothing seemed to stop me from this insatiable desire to get my ministerial license. See Matthew 16:18. I continued studying day and night working to complete those six courses. The Lord even blessed me, with a dependable computer to assist me in my drive for Excellency in study. The first course of Homiletics, I started on in May, and I completed the required five remaining course by the end of December. I take no credit for this whatever, To God Be All the Glory, Honor, and Praise. It was Him through me that allowed me to do just what He apparently had ordained. Well no words could explain how I felt. The business ran itself, with the help of my one employee. Income had never been better. If I needed a thousand dollars to pay bills it was there. If I needed fifteen hundred dollars to pay bills it was there. See Isaiah 65:24. All, I wanted do was study. I would type from dawn to night working many times (12 to 15) hours a day, on these courses, and The Holy Spirit would seemingly feed me the input for each and every lesson, I was involved with. To give an example, I was discussing with a pastor friend from Johnson Chapel about my courses, and he began to tell me about the time while being enrolled in ministry school, of how he was requested to write something about the Psalm 23. Not knowing what to write, he wrote it in negative fashion instead of writing, "The Lord Is My Shepherd," he wrote it, "The Lord Is Not My Shepherd." He said it turned out to be a masterpiece for which he received a good grade. Strangely enough within just a short time, I had the same assignment. Like him, I would not have known what to write about, but with this input, I proceeded to write it in the same manner.

By now it was the year 94, and I was making plans to go on another mission trip to Africa, but I did not allow my attention to be diverted from my course of studies. It was as though they were an integral part of me.

See John 10:10, By now: the last of February, had arrived and it was time to go again to the annual prophecy conference. Being the special event that it was, we made this our annual vacation, and a time to draw closer to our Lord. Again the Good Lord supplied the means to go. By the time we returned from the conference in Florida, we had just about two weeks to catch up on some studies, before leaving again this time on a (19) day trip to Sierra Leona W. Africa. There is something about laboring for the master that can't be replaced with anything this world has to offer.

LITTLE IS MUCH, WHEN GOD IS IN IT

1. In the harvest field now ripened, there's a work for all to do: hark, the voice of God is calling, to the harvest calling you.

2. Does the place you're called to labor seem so small and little known? It is great if God is in it, And He'll not forget His own.

3. When the conflict here is ended and our race on earth is run: He will say if we are faithful, welcome home, my child, well done.

4. When we enter Heaven's portals And our Savior's face we; see; Cares of life will be forgotten, we'll be happy, glad, and free.

Chorus—Little is much when God is in it, Labor not for wealth or fame;
There's a crown and you can win it. If you go in Jesus' name.

Having returned from Africa, again we had some speaking engagements, but
for the most part continued to cram, and burn the midnight oil. We had targeted
the end of September to finish our (24) course two year associate ministerial
degree. I was well on time in doing so, completing two courses a month. Based
on this, I was allowed to stand with the graduating class of (94).

Shortly after returning from Africa, I received a mailer from God's News,
reference, a "Jerusalem Prophecy Conference," to be held October, (94). My
first reaction when reading the mailer was Wow! What a place to have a prophecy
conference, the city of all cities, "The City Of God." But I rejected the idea, in
as much as I had already been to Florida for a whole week, Africa for 19 days,
and had not worked more than a week to date. Laying it aside, I forgot about
it.

My business had exploded on every operable front, yet seemingly without my
participation. The car sales lot, the rental business, the in house beauty shop, and
now the chance for the wife to manage a nursing home beauty shop with a salary.

I still had my sights on finishing the courses by the end of September, and I
was well on track. Mid August came, and I received a call from an unknown
farmer wanting to have a farm sale. With my studies on track for completion in
September, I refused knowing that it might hinder that finish date. The farmer
was rather insistent, and so with reluctance, I scheduled a meeting with him, for
the second time, having canceled the first time. When finally making contact with
him, and going over the criterion for the auction, it did not seem worth while
causing me to set a minimum fee, of one hundred dollars. The auction business
is not without competition, and it would have been easy for the owner to find
another auctioneer, but the Lord, I believe was in charge. Having made all the
necessary arrangements, I studied right up to sale time. When arriving at the sale
sight, there were no parking spaces available. It seemed as though the whole
county had shown up for the sale.

When tallying up the day's receipts, it ended up being one of the largest sales,
commission wise, that I had ever had.

The following day, while finishing the expense related work for the sale, I was
leafing through a stack of invoices, and up pops the brochure about the
Jerusalem Prophecy Conference. The wording literally jumped out at me. The

final confirmation date for trip was two days past, but something said call. When calling the receptionist stated that the trip had just been shut down for any new tourist, but she believed I could still get signed up. She told me to call her back in one half hour. Doing so, I was able to book a trip to the Holy Land, scheduled for October. Had it not been for the large auction sale, I would not have been able to go. Well I was ecstatic.

Now it seemed as though God was making it possible for me to see everything that I had studied about for the past months.

Well needless to say, I worked at fever pitch with more drive than ever to complete the courses on time. Much to my surprise I finished, what I thought was my last course September 15.

ISRAEL BOUND

Beyond what I read in the Bible I knew very little about Israel. The touring company sent me a number of maps, and informational packages pertaining to the upcoming trip, giving me time to acquaint myself with each area of our tour. For some unknown reason, I begin to feel a tremendous love for the Jewish people, like I had ever known. And with each passing day, it increased.

I had fifteen days before leaving for Israel, so I spent my spare time around the car lot, and house taking care of some various business. I couldn't wait till October 1, date of departure. All the while my love for Israel and its people begin to surge in me to heights that I had trouble containing.

It seemed as though, I was in the jiggle mode of a pressure cooker, spiritually speaking. I felt as though I could just blow up.

Since accepting Jesus, He has always been bigger than Life itself, and continues to be bigger and bigger as one follows Him. I couldn't help but think of a silly analogy to identify with that. None other than the silly bionic man on television who seemingly would walk around in normal mode, until someone would happen to tick him off, and with that, he would start swelling up, bursting his buttons, off of his shirt, and pants and then would go on a rampage. Sometimes that's the way one feels when getting so full of God that you just can't contain.

ON THE WAY TO THE HOLY LAND

Well the day arrived for me to go to Israel, and My, What a joyous time, it was. As we winged our way out over the North Atlantic Ocean towards Jerusalem "The Power, of God," seemed to magnify itself more by the mile. When arriving our destination, the surreal Power, and presence of God, was so powerfully felt, that it seemed as though one could cut it with a knife. For the next ten days (a story all of its own) we toured the historical, and splendiferous sights of The Nation of Israel, seeing, and living everything that I had studied about the last fourteen months. What a glorious time it was. When one can stand on the Mount Of Olives and remember the angel's words, "YE MEN OF GALLILEE," or can tour the Garden Tomb, at the foot of Mount Calvary, or the Garden Of Gethsemane, where He sweat great drops of blood, for the lost and dying worlds behalf, It's hard to have dry eyes. At our departure, the entire entourage of tourist, including myself, left different then we came, each having a greater revelation of Jesus Christ, and His Kingdom.

Returning from our trip, I made contact with the University, for an update on my overall grade average. Much to my surprise, they advised, that I had somehow missed the course of Bible History. By now I was out of the study mode, that I had been so involved with the last fourteen months, but God gave me the enabling power, to complete this course in the same timely manner as the others. The abundance of literature I had obtained from Israel helped me greatly to authenticate the course work. In a total of fourteen months, God through me, allowed me, to complete all twenty four courses, in a record length of time with a (A-) average. Only God could have done that. I take no credit for this at all. I only state this, to bring Honor, and Glory, to The Lord Jesus. Likewise this along with a one year mentoring program through a Church was a necessary prerequisite for an associate ministerial degree, and the ordination certificate.

TIME TO PUT INTO PRACTICE

Well now it was time to put into practice what I had studied the last fourteen months. At a dinner the church prepared for me following the trip in Israel, I shall never forget, one staunch member of the church, ask me; well "Bill what are your plans now that you are out of ministry school?" I said; "well at present I am going to divest myself of all my business activity, and get involved with ministry fulltime." That seemed almost a natural for me, as nothing else really mattered.

Well I still had the former bankruptcy in mind to deal with. How could I stand before the multitudes of people owing, money. Creditors are like elephants. If you once file bankruptcy on them even though you make it good they always remember it. Since filing in the early 90's I had worked, as it were with one hand tied behind my back. Not good with the business I was involved with. Even though God had graciously provided, I didn't have the barrowing power I once had, limiting my projected goals. But now my goals were totally different than before. Earlier I had sought to build my own kingdom, now I was only interested in helping to build God's Kingdom. By now, I had amassed several pieces of Real Estate, and the businesses that I had mentioned earlier, but it had little or no meaning to me. Little by little I begin to dismantle the total operation.

I had received my first student license with the Holiness Church, and had started my one year mentoring program under the direction of our pastor.

While appearing before the Holiness District Board for affirmation of license, they had become aware of my continued liquidation of business assets. They posed the question of reasoning behind my actions, pertaining to liquidation, and I responded, "I hardly see how I could evict someone today, or repossess their vehicle today and then try to effectively minister to them tomorrow." "I don't believe it could be done."

I had become so hardened with this type activity that I didn't give a care about any one.

This reply, brought an abrupt laughter, and later some serious discussion, and I am sure some serious soul searching, from within that board room that day. For many of them were in the same shoes.

I earlier had posed the same question to a so called preacher that I was knowledgeable about, who, like me, had amassed a far greater number of rentals then what I had. When I ask what he did about evictions, etc. reference his ministry he stated, "Well praise God we win a few, and we lose a few." God help us! That is the way I had become, now I wanted no part of it.

START OF MINISTRY, LOSS OF LICENSE

From time to time I begin to have opportunities to speak in some Holiness churches. Likewise I was still enrolled in the mentoring program. I was involved with the local jail ministry, to a degree, but was limited because of having a student-ministers license. Likewise I was unable to perform weddings. And still yet, I did not speak with any degree of regularity. That troubled me in the worst way. Because of my disobedience to God, in my earlier years, I had been forced to wear ten different hats of occupations, never reaching the pinnacle of success in any one area, and now my efforts still seemed to be stymied in what I felt so sure about. My prayer night, and day, Lord help me get speaking engagements.

Following my licensure with the Holiness Church, I toured the main headquarters of the church, acquainting myself with the various ministry programs, and their district leaders. Much discussion was made reference the establishment of an independent ministry for the purpose of having crusades, of which I have always had interest. I was not sure of their stance towards such an endeavor, but found them to be receptive, and helpful.

For the next few weeks, I feverishly worked on the corporate 501 c charter, a necessary prerequisite for the establishment of any private ministry. This provides for the tax exempt status through local, state, and federal officials. Through the IRS, I was given a five year trial period. And I proceeded.

I modeled my charter after the Holiness Churches practically one hundred percent for I have always been in league with their fundamental beliefs.

Albeit when attempting to use the same language reference the section pertaining to "The GIFTS OF THE HOLY SPIRIT," I was checked by "The HOLY SPIRIT." I was not sure why, but I could not proceed, as they had.

I scheduled a meeting with my mentor, and pastor discussing with him, The Holiness views, of the church, reference the GIFTS. I had watched men like Ron Pugh many times, and they seemed to have services unlike anything that I had observed in our church. I personally had observed him many times knocking people to the floor, speaking in unknown language, telling people about their future, it seemed to go on and on. In light of our own church discipline, it didn't make any sense, and worse yet my mentor couldn't tell me anything of value about it. The only thing he could give me was the churches view.

Still yet that did not satisfy my conscience and so I ended up putting in my charter a line, with the wording: (I didn't know anything about the Gifts of the Holy Spirit, but I would pray and seek God's Face about Them) I gave the district officials a copy of my completed charter, and they didn't seem to have any problems with it.

With the charter in force, I begin to work with the next problem my student licensure. As I alluded to earlier we could not get into the jails except on routine visitation hours. This was family time, and inmates were reluctant to use it for ministerial purposes.

I was still a year or so away from getting my ordination license,

As stated earlier, I had always tried to be prepared in the best manner possible, for the task at hand likewise, should I not do the same for the cause of Christ.

I didn't give it a second thought. Having searched the church manual, I saw no restriction for a second license, and so in error, or providentially, not knowing the outcome, "I chose to believe the latter," I committed the unthinkable, so far as the Church was concerned. I applied for an interim license from a reputable ministry, of like faith. Following several interviews, and the perusal of school transcripts, they offered me that interim license. They were made aware of the reasoning involved. The understanding was that this license would be in effect until receiving my ordination through the Holiness Church. When telling my mentor, of my interim ordination certificate, because of an upcoming wedding, he immediately called a board meeting, and promptly dismissed me from the mentoring program within the church. He did not tell me in person, but chose to have the district board to notify me. He later told me that he felt as though, I had kicked him in the gut. He felt that I was trying to side step the ordination requirements. No amount of explanation would reconcile him.

The district board, deactivated my current license, and revoked my upcoming license. When appearing before the board, "many, being my lifelong friends," I asked if I might return to the program. And they gave me this option.

1. Surrender my interim license by certified mail, meaning, that I would have no license, as they had revoked my student license.

2. I would need a favorable vote from the local church board, and then the church body,

3. If that all went well then I would need to return to the district board for a favorable vote. And they let it be known that they did not take kindly to one doing as I had done, and would not guarantee me a license.

They had all but shut the door. I was devastated to say the least. I felt like I was shot out of the saddled before I ever got started. That decision was rendered on Saturday, and on Monday, I called Dr. Scott a member of the board, my long time friend, and ask him if they, had said, what I thought they had said. Despite the friendship he didn't give me much encouragement, or any other options.

For the next several months, the wife and I suffered rejection unthinkable. They would hardly give us the time of day. All speaking engagements were canceled. The devil only shot himself: in the foot, for if anything this rejection and suspension of license only strengthened my resolve. It was just another test to bring me into the position God wanted me.

The ministry, my interim license was with allowed me to keep them permanently.

In the earlier part of this fiasco, I was subjected too much temptation, reference bitterness, but God, in His Infinite Wisdom enabled me to overcome.

See 1 Corinthians 10:13 I was later asked: "Are you not bitter at your friends and the church board for their decision?" I replied; "no."

Somehow, God had given me a special love, for those on that board, who seemed to be so obstinate, to the precarious predicament I was in, and if anything I appreciated the courage they had, in standing against me (a long time friend), in favor of the church, even though it went against me. God had carried me through this dark time of our life preparing more than ever for the future that lied ahead. Isn't God good, See PSALMs: 91

Well within six to eight months the local church and pastor, my former mentor reconciled with me, and from that point on I spoke a number of times, within several Holiness Churches, including my own. God has a way of healing.

ON OUR JOURNEY IN THE RV

Our final business day was October 31, 96.

We had successfully liquidated all of our real estate with the exception of our personal dwelling, and one rental which needed to be remodeled. We still had one remaining closure our (car lot building, a former service station), which seemingly was being held up because of government regulations, reference buried tanks. I had obtained documentation of tank removal, but that did not satisfy the lender.

The buyer was as disgruntled as I was, because he wanted that building to house his rental office in. It was located on one of the busiest intersections of the city.

Over the written objections of his attorney, he opted to pay me cash, as opposed to using a lending institution. Just another example of God having his hand on me enabling me to do what He had called me to do. If it had not been for a cash buyer, only God knows what would have happened to that building.

With money in hand, we were set to go on the road.

Our private home was rented to a unique tenant. The remaining rental was awaiting renovation.

Purchasing a RV, we moved our possessions into it and headed south to Florida, for the long awaited prophecy conference, and our usual week of vacation. Following the conference we returned to the daughter's house for a short time, and then returned to Indiana, for renovation of our rental. When finished we relocated to southern Indiana allowing us to be in close proximity to our remaining rentals. Wife and I had fully intended to stay in this area for some time, but something still was amiss, we seemed to be wondering aimlessly. I still was not speaking with any degree of regularity, a major concern, all of its own. Retirement funds only last so long.

For some reason we felt a pull, or a drawing to return to Tennessee, and so following a Sunday night speaking engagement, we again made our way back to Tennessee. God seemed to be calling us to this area, for what reasons we did not know. Strangely enough our daughter had only lived in this area for one year, but they too were providentially drawn to this area. Nothing appeared to be special about this area, as it is far from most of the major tourist attractions, yet for reasons unknown, they chose it. Had they not moved to this location, we would not have known about it.

By now it was the spring of 98, and I still was speaking with little degree of regularity. Wife and I started attending a small Baptist church in the immediate area, and after a few weeks started speaking on occasion, yet it was void of any futuristic plans.

While roaming, ATB had become a very necessary part of our life. I will always be grateful to its founders Betty and Jim Roth, and the overall ATB family, for they are a Godsend to the entire world.

Over the years, it had been our church when for one reason or another we couldn't be involved with a church. I still believe it to be one of the most fertile (soul producing) ministries one can sow seed to.

No words could ever express the encouragement I have always received from the myriad of miraculous faith stories that Jim and Betty Roth share reference the founding of their ministry. And God's miraculous provisions, continues to flow in an unprecedented manner.

The encouragement one receives from ATB is certainly worth every dollar one can give, in its support. It had become a major tool, God used to guide us in our limited faith walk to date, and more widely used to guide us in a new Faith Covenant Relationship God was beginning to bring us into.

Our desires and our prayers had been for fulltime ministry, as I had alluded to earlier,

But little if any results were occurring or in evidence. And now for one reason or another, I felt an obsession, or an over whelming urge to just give God everything.

It could not have happened at a better time, for by now the spring 98 ATB Praise-a-thon was on. As always there were many faith stories, from God's faithful faith warriors. And unlike before I seemingly took more interest in them perhaps because of my own circumstances. The idea of giving to get was not in the vocabulary of the traditional fundamental church I had come from. In many ways they believed in God's blessing but not to the extent, as I heard on ATB. It fascinated me. God seemingly had prepared the wife and I for this time, for by now we had all but exhausted our retirements funds, we had $2300.00 remaining.

BEGINNING, 5-20-98, A FULL COMMITMENT

On this date we made the commitment to plant the last $2000.00 we had in Gods ministry at ATB. We did so with fear and trepidation. We retained the last $300.00 to pay some bills with. 05-21-98 we followed thru with commitment. On this date we purchased a cashier's check for the $2000.00 and sent it to ATB.

We expected a miracle immediately, and in many ways we received one. See Isaiah 29:14. We received no money to replace the $2000.00 we had just planted. Needless to say the remaining $300.00 was not sufficient to handle our bills. Our trust was in the Lord and remembering the way that He had provided for us earlier, we decided we would play it to the end. Little by little as the bills came in, and in an effort to salvage our rebuilt credit reputation, we begin to sell off what few items we had left, enabling us to stay afloat.

While we did not realize it at the time, the painful transition from total dependence upon our self to total dependence upon God was occurring.

For the last six years since coming to know Christ our incomes had never been better. Our lives had never been fuller. We had often Praised' and thank God for allowing us to, have more, do more, and go more than at any other time in our life. Now it had all come to a grinding halt, not to mention of our rebuilt credit reputation which seemed to be going down the drain, with everything else.

The only thing that seemed to be getting better was our relationship with Christ. The continual presence of God and his inner still small voice saying "TRUST ME, I KNOW WHAT I AM DOING," continued on. See Proverbs 3:5-6

Well somehow God continued to give us the strength, and resolve to continue. By now all of our bills were in arrears, driving us more and more to our knees. We tried to keep them as solvent as possible, but with little success. Finally in our moment of desperation we decided to pawn our car hauling trailer, in hopes of redemption, receiving about twenty five percent of what we had paid for it, just before going on the road. This kept us in funds, but still yet in short supply. See Romans 4:17,

More over my mind continually reflected on how God had provided for us earlier while in ministry school, in liquidation of assets especially the car lot building, even in my mother estate.

Well Satan loves to cloud the focus, and this time certainly was no exception. But somehow I knew in my knower, in my inner being, (to use Dr. Roth's remarks) that I had a call to preach.

I believed that He had already provided me ample evidence for that end, and I was not about to be deterred.

By now my former bankruptcy, and my diminished loss of credibility do to the recent circumstances, had become a real burden to me.

I want to strongly emphasize, that no one thought more of a credit reputation then me. I often bragged about it. And quite frankly I believe the mark of a good Christian is to pay his bills on time. I had always tried to do just that but for some unknown reason, now I wasn't able to do that.

In times past I had every conceivable back up plan possible to prevent, such as this from happening yet, all of my backups seemingly disappeared quicker then what I could control. There clearly was a force greater than me at work. I didn't understand it. Did I not have an obligation to my creditors, as a Christian much less a minister.

06-98, ATTENDED PENTECOST TENT REVIVAL AT WATER TOWN

In early July 98 on a Sunday afternoon the daughter needed to make a run into Water Town to the K-Mart store. I detest these type stores especially on Sunday but the wife and I decided to ride with them. Earlier I had noticed a tent, RV., and trailer like I had, setting next door to the K-Mart plaza. While they went shopping, I went snooping. Going to the sight I was able to speak with the Rev. Steele. He turned out to be the Pastor of The New Beginning Worship Center at Pearl City, Tn.

He was a very friendly and charismatic individual to say the least. After the standard pleasantries, I enquired of the reason for the tent. He explained they were having a tent revival. I begin to tell him some details of my ministry, and of my RV and trailer which was similar to his. After a fair length conversation he invited me to his church at Pearl City to speak on a Wednesday night. I accepted, and then he invited me to the tent revival that night.

I left happy that I had received another speaking engagement. When returning, I told the wife, of the tent revival but because of the extreme temperature, she wanted to go to the church that we had been attending regularly because of the air conditioning. After a few rounds of words we finally ended up going to the tent revival.

We were in for a surprise. I had never been to a service of that nature. It was similar in nature to what I had enquired of, when talking with my mentor, reference the gifts of The Holy Spirit, referred to earlier.

I had seen Ron Pugh do the same thing, on TV, now I was seeing it live. There was life in that church that I hadn't seen for years. Singing, shouting, dancing, clapping, preaching, and then the unthinkable, the minister that night following his sermon came over to me and begin to tell me everything about me that no one could know, except I told them. And then he prayed over me. Likewise when he returned to the pulpit he started laying hands on people, as if to knock them down. And then they would start speaking in this funny language what I learned later to be the Heavenly language. I was so startled by his revelation to me, that I went to the pastor, who I had talked with earlier, and ask him if he had told the evangelist about me. He said: "no, I have not had a chance to talk with him."

I said: "how would he know such things?" he replied: "that's word of knowledge and wisdom." Well let me tell you for the next few weeks I saw some strange things Luke 5:26

Well strangely enough before all this occurred probably six to eight weeks earlier, I had somehow injured my back causing me to walk on crutches, from time to time. Even that condition was totally healed, in one of the services, by the pastor laying hands on me. From that night on we never missed another service for over two years. It was always so refreshing. It was as though God was showing me everything, that I had enquired of my mentor and the only response he could give was The Holiness Church View. Mark 7:13

Following the seven day tent revival, we started attending The New Beginning Worship Center. I still was amazed at the strange happenings, and quite frankly, I didn't understand it, but whatever it was, I wanted.

Within the Holiness Church I was saved and had received, the second work of grace, referred to as Sanctification. Was this now, a third work of grace? The Holiness Church seemed to deny this, or at least pretend that there is nothing to speaking, in The Heavenly Language. Many ministers have been defrocked for being involved in any way with Pentecost. Yet one stanch Member of the church I left, The Mrs. Lotus, expressed her opinion one time that she believed there was a higher plain then what perhaps the church was teaching but she never elaborated, perhaps not knowing what it was.

Well for the next several weeks I begin to seek God's face reference the Baptism of The Holy Spirit, and then one night at church, He answer my prayer. Well words cannot express my feeling reference the Baptism of the Holy Spirit. See Luke 24:49

Well as is written in Luke, that was just what I felt like. I felt as if I could just blow up.

Yet despite the remarkable improvements, I seemed to be making in my spiritual walk, my finances seem to be deteriorating more and more.

BY SAYING THIS I DON'T WANT TO DIMINISH GOD'S PROMISIES OF PROVISION AS I WILL EXPLAIN LATER

I didn't understand it. We now were beginning to run totally empty again so far as cash. The proceeds from my trailer had dwindled. While I paid cash for my RV., I had even picked up some EXTRA cash on my RV and now it was even beginning to run delinquent. I seemingly had nowhere to turn, yet when I prayed the Lord reminded me, in His still small voice, "Trust Me I Know What I Am Doing."

Comforting yet perplexing.

At the point of desperation, the wife and I decided, that we would go to work at Goodies. That lasted for two weeks. What a mistake. We both had been acclimated, to self employment all of our life, retiring from that arena, and now here we were trying to work for a few measly dollars just to get by. In desperation we both quit. Were we lazy? I think not. I had a firm commitment that somehow I was going to see this ministry come through. That's when I decided that I would leave the area and perhaps do something, I didn't know what.

I didn't understand what was going on. Well the Lord had other plans, for as I started to leave the RV blew up. Everything that could go wrong with that RV did go wrong with it. The cabinetry begin to come loose, the air conditioning unit failed, the awning was ripped loose, the outer skin begin to separate from the body, forgetting to put the TV antenna down, I knocked it off in my haste leaving, the clutch fan went out for the third time, and the straw that broke the camel's back was the refrigerator went out. Although it was late fall, hot weather was still prevalent forcing us to at least make a decision about the refrigerator. They were unable to find a part to repair it, and the insurance we had purchased for such problems refused to replace it. With little or no money to make the needed repairs, we opted to sell it. RV's are like houses, they require special financing. Without dealer assistance it doesn't happen. The dealer whom we had went to for repairs, and estimates etc. offered me about 50% of what I had paid for the thing February 97. We both enjoyed the RV, and this was the last thing we both wanted, but felt we had no choice. We accepted our loss and started making other arrangement, for housing. Immediately we were confronted with high rent, no furniture, and even the availability of housing. It was something God had to work out. God seemed to guide our every move. Until finding a place we moved into a single room motel at The Inn of Lenore City. Although a bit crowded, it was sufficient. It was far from what we had planned, but somehow we felt peace, and contentment. At least we had some money.

Despite the seemingly endless obstacles Satan was throwing at us, our resolve grew stronger than ever, and our call to ministry seemed to burn that much more within me. By now Christmas time, had arrived, and management for the Knoxville water front, was advertising for a Christmas boat parade to be held on the Tennessee River. Sat. Nov. 21, 98. This was a new experience for us, as our rivers, in Indiana, are frozen over at this time of year preventing such activity. The wife and I decided that we would take the grandbabies to see the boat parade. When arriving for the parade we learned that it would follow a VOLS football game playing a few blocks from the waterfront. Following the game the fans begin to gather for the parade, half inebriated, singing, and screaming out in mockery, and drunken revelry, the sacred Christmas carols the band was playing.

SILENT NIGHT, HOLY NIGHT, that was far from their thoughts that night.

1. Silent Night Holy Night, All is calm, all is bright, Round yon Virgin Mother and Child! Holy infant so tender and mild, Sleep in Heavenly peace, Sleep in Heavenly peace.

2. Silent Night, Holy Night! Shepherds quake at the sight, Glories stream from Heaven afar, Heavenly Hosts sing Alleluia; Christ the Savior is born, Christ the Savior is born.

3. Silent Night, Holy Night, Son of God, loves pure light, radiant beams, from Thy Holy face, with the dawn of Redeeming Grace, Jesus Lord at Thy birth, Jesus, Lord at Thy Birth.

I was heart sick for my Lord. One cannot have a relationship with Jesus Christ and here His name cursed, or mocked without feeling, sick. Needless to say we did not stay around to enjoy the parade.

When returning to the Inn, I was heart sick. By now we had been in the Inn for close to a month and with the high rents in this area it looked as if we might be there several months but again God had

Different, plans for us.

DREAM

Little did I know what still lay ahead that night, I was broken hearted over the happenings at the parade, I retired but couldn't sleep for the heart break, I, felt for the Master. I literally hugged my pillar tight against my face, and as God is my witness I felt as though I was stroking the Masters hair. I went in to a deep sob, saying to Him, I am sorry, I am sorry for you for all of the mockery and drunken reveling that occurred.

I just laid there, seemingly for some time, holding as it were His head in my arms, and then I cried saying: "Lord I have done everything I know, to get started in this ministry but I am no further ahead than I was when I started." "I have exhausted all of what I thought I had in knowhow, and come to find out I knew nothing." "I have exhausted all of my retirement funds, and still I have no ministry."

I literally ended up crying myself to sleep. Sometime within the next few hours whether by dream, or vision, I cannot tell. I came into this room, for which I perceived to be a room near Heaven, for the second time. This time there were three men standing with long gray, and dark red robes. As I entered, they begin to laugh, and as I stood there, someone came from behind me, and put His hands on my waist, and started lifting me to the ceiling.

The higher I went, the louder they all laughed, and the one lifting me, was laughing just as hard and loud. It was the most joyous, and joyful laughter, that I had ever heard, and I begin to laugh with them, and all of sudden I begin to slowly come down, startled, I turned to see who it was, and there He was "THE LORD JESUS," He said something to me in the HEAVENLY LANGUAGE (He later revealed it to be: "Everything Is Going To Be Alright."

45

MY SAVIOR FIRST OF ALL

1. When my lives work is ended, and I cross the swelling tide, When the bright and glorious morning I shall see, I shall know my redeemer, when I reach the other side, And His smile will be to welcome me.

2. Oh the soul thrilling rapture when I view His blessed face, and the luster of His kindly beaming eyes, how my full heart will praise Him, for the mercy, love and grace that prepare for me, a mansion in the sky.

3. Oh the dear ones in glory how they beckon me to come, And our parting at the river, I recall, to the sweet vales of Eden, they will sing my welcome home, But I long to meet my Savior first of all.

4. Thru the gates to the city, in the robe of spotless white, He will lead me where no tears will ever fall; in the glad song of ages, I shall mingle with delight, But I long to meet my Savior first of All

Chorus I shall know Him, I shall know Him, and redeemed by His side, I shall stand, I shall know Him, I shall know Him, by the print of the nails in His hand.

When awaking, I didn't know what to think. I didn't know whether to tell anyone, for fear they would think I was crazy but I couldn't keep it still.

That was on Saturday night, and on Monday, of the following week, I was able to move into an affordable apartment, for ($225.00) per month. We still needed furniture, when starting to buy some, The Lord said: "Let me worry about the furniture." Within a week we had a complete apartment, full of furniture. Just in time for Christmas.

THE YEAR 1999—FINANCES AGAIN, PROBLEM WITH OUR RENTAL

The same time we moved to the Inn of Lenoir City, I received word from the tenant, that our furnace had went bad at our former residence, Frankfort, IN. With no money, and no credit, we didn't know what to do, but then all of a sudden God seemingly resurrected ones to help us out, through the company where we had purchased the furnace and that paid for the furnace repair. Well over ($400.00).

By now the Christmas season was upon us, and The Lord provided for us, a beautiful Christmas.

By now, I was becoming quite involved with The New Beginning Worship Center. We attended regularly, and lived with in close proximity to the church, providing me a prayer closet. It was during these times that I begin to know the meaning of Psalm 46:10.

I had never done this before. I always did all the talking, but never gave much thought to God, talking to me, beyond what little He, had before.

In earlier times, He seemed to be guiding me more into full time ministry. But audible instructions, was never to my knowledge, used, and yet at the same time, He seemed to be able to get messages across to me as needed, i.e. in answer to my many prayers. While I can't say, God audibly told me, it seemed as though, He was saying: "Have at the ministry fulltime, see if you can trust me for it"

Now, in the quite times, alone before God, on the church floor, as I would lay there, from time to time, The Lord would seemingly talk to me in a way that I can't explain. It was as though, He spoke to me by putting given thoughts in my mind at a fast pace, so strong that I would just speak them with my lips, with no help from me. This occurred several times before I really begin to take notice of it. I would try from time to time to mimic, as it were, the fast paced thoughts running through my mind, but come to learn, that I couldn't even think that fast.

As earlier stated, we were at ground zero so far as finance goes. The money we received from the sale of the RV., was no more than enough to keep us in the most needful things, nothing to pay on any of the bills, now long overdue.

Over and over I searched the scriptures, and prayed continually about this unseemly situation, yet there seemed to be no reduction of onslaught, from Satan. Was I wrong? Had I been mislead? Thousands of questions came to mind, to erode my thinking in believing and trusting God.

How could I stand before the world and preach the Gospel with such problems? The secular world said, go to work, and believe me many of our friends by now were quick to express their feelings in this regard. Human logic says go to work, Divine logic says Trust God. And that seemed to be what God was telling me. As talked about so much on ATB, I was, believing, God, for a miracle of debt repayment, and or, cancellation, reference my previous bankruptcy, from which I had partially recovered, but had never been able to repay anyone. Now these current financial happenings were none the better. Somehow that just didn't seem right.

By now more and more promises came through revelation. Matthew 6:33 came in to focus, more than ever.

I was determined that nothing would, or could deter me, from what I felt, God had called me to do. Somehow I could not reconcile getting a job. It just didn't seem right. I struggled with the earlier thought, I felt God had given me "Have at It! see if you can trust me for it," and that seemed to set the stage for my behavior reference secular employment.

I wanted to stay in the light of God's glory, and for me to be involved with a fulltime job seemed to distract me from that.

By now, spring was upon us, and time had come, for The Knoxville Prayer Summit. I wanted to attend it, if at all possible. It consisted of a group of ministers getting together, for five days, in a mountain retreat and seeking Gods face for the duration of time.

At the same time, I had a chance to take a census job, which was more along my line of work, and chose at least to take the training. There again as I set in training for a solid week of indoctrination, it took me out of that critical vain of thought, that I had persisted upon staying in since I left Indiana 10-96

I purposed again, despite Hell and high water, that I would not let anything deter me from Mt.6:33, so I abruptly quit and prepared to go to the prayer summit.

In the mean time, the church invited a prophet by the name of John Nash to come to the church for services. Following his message, he called the wife, and I, to the front, to prophesy over us. He stated: "That we were going to have a great ministry, but before that, we would have many chances to sell out." He concluded with the admonishment: "Don't do it, for you will never be sorry." The wife and I left that service happy, but wondering what on earth could he be talking about.

Well within a short period of time we begin to find out.

By now, with The Lord's help we were beginning to see some bench marks for which I believe, The Lord was faithful to provide, to help us in our faith walk.

BENCH MARK ONE—Creditors seemed to be held at bay.

BENCH MARK TWO—En route from one of the organizational meetings pertaining to the summit, I was riding with the pastor of New Beginning, and two other Pastors in the back seat. While riding I overheard Don Lamb, ask Joe Weise, "Well how is things going?" Joe responded: "You have heard of the film, To Hell and back, "That's where I have been this last year. I am just now beginning to get some of my credibility back." I, am not in the habit of listening to other people's conversations, but somehow, I believe God, allowed me to be privy to that conversation, to let me know, that ministers, even High Dollar, well thought of Ministers such as Joe, are subject to losing their credibility, just as I had, for whatever reason. Well, that seemed to put a crimp in the devils mouth, for he had told me, that I had sin in my life, and that I wasn't suppose to preach.

BENCH MARK THREE—One day while watching our beloved ATB, Dr. Whittenburg came on the set, telling the story, of his demise, following his conversion, and call to ministry, saying, that in his walk with God, for some unknown reason, he was forced to go, from a $550,000.00 house, down to a $40,000.00 double wide. One can only imagine the problems surrounding such a, demise.

BENCH MARK FOUR—Again at another prayer summit organizational meeting one black minister, "stated that he was called to take over a church, in the Knoxville area, and just shortly before his arrival, the church (had several thousand members, and expenses to fit the needs of that size congregation), but somehow through a church split the church was left with just over 200 members, no money in the bank, and $50,000.00 interest alone was owed to the mortgage company. And if that was not enough, so much arrearage on utilities were due, and owing, that they had to worship in the dark. And the minister stated for the next six months following his employment with the church, the more they prayed the worse things got. He said a few months following his tenure that he would have left in a heartbeat but didn't have enough money or gas in the car to get out of town. (That sounded very familiar). WAS GOD TRYING TO TELL ME SOMETHING?

BENCH MARK FIVE—One year to the day of commitment, I was asked to be Assistant Pastor of New Beginning. And in addition, I received the first faith money, for my needs.

I immediately took over the church van route, and the wife cleaned the church. At about the same time, I was also involved with the local jail ministry, and nursing home ministry. Since the incident at the Inn, God had elevated my speaking engagements from next to nothing to ten to twelve times per month.

We continued in this capacity from May 20, 1999 to Aug 22, 2000. Much of the time, the wife, and I was working 6 to 10 hours a day, calling, counseling, teaching, hospital visitation, wife cleaning church, driving church van, and later established a discipleship class. This was one of the most enjoyable years of my life, and the first time ever, my wife begged me to stay home with her, instead of calling or doing church business. Much of that year, the pastor was away in evangelism giving us full control of the church except Sundays for which he would return. It seemed to be a perfect arrangement, for both the pastor, and me, giving me the privilege of receiving my ordination through a Pentecostal denomination, following a, year tenure as the assistant pastor.

Now God was telling me: "I didn't call you out of the business world, for you to get back in secular employment, but to be involved with my ministry full time."

I was trusting, Him, for a full time ministry, now, He was telling me this.

While I had felt that way I can't remember God ever telling me that.

I have learned many things since coming into Pentecost, but perhaps one of the most important things I have learned, is:

Not to express need. See quote at end of Book.

We have always been careful not to let our needs be known.

Although we were involved fulltime as the assistant pastor, we did not receive any stable salary. Still yet we had no income, beyond what people gave us in love offerings, and that was limited.

We stayed afloat through Sept 99, partially from proceeds arrived from the sale of our RV., But now our funds had diminished to nothing, and with no salary we were beginning to enter another severe testing time.

BUILDING FAITH AND TRUST IN JESUS

Sooner or later one will be required to lean totally on Jesus, or get out of the boat and walk with Him in deep water, as some of the faith ministers call it.

Revelations to date:

1. No, secular employment, and fulltime ministry.
2. Be, still and know that I am God,
3. Have at it! See if you can trust me for a fulltime ministry.
4. Now God was telling me through Daniel 4:35 that men do what God, Wills

And In revelation to me The Lord had coined a phrase "FAITH, LOVE, AND OBEDIENCE, WRAPPED IN A GARMENT OF PRAISE."

Up until this time, my needs were met by attrition of all of my personal things, including the RV, Trailer, and Key Board that I had purchased for the ministry. The only thing that I had left at that time was two computers, some tools, plus the furniture the Lord had given us.

Doing a plumbing job, for our Pastor, ignoring god's command, of, ministry only, and with finance still in short supply, I chose to do a plumbing job for the pastor on one of his rentals.

The job turned out to be a thorn in my flesh. The sub contractor misread the transit readings, like, wise, I became sick, forcing me to rely on non skilled help, to complete the job. Needless to say the job had to be redone. Consequently it cost me all of my tools. This was a very hard lesson.

10-99 first month rent missed.

The Lord began to deal with me, reference, writing a check for rent. The last two months that I had paid rent it was rather strenuous to say the least consequently forcing me to sell more items to cover the check. He made it clear He didn't want me to rely on the two to three day grace period one can generally have (with great risk) by writing a check. So with much reluctance I chose to obey.

Well being the former Landlord I was, and having no money for which to pay the rent, I advised the Management of my inability to pay the rent. Being the first time I was late she had little concern. As I told her I wasn't sure what was going on but I believed God would come through for me. She just told me to stay in contact with her. By the middle of the month, I became real concerned bombarding heaven daily with my whys. Always the same answer TRUST ME, I KNOW WHAT I AM DOING, MEN, DO WHAT I WILL. At this particular time that was of very little encouragement, yet I knew I had to Trust Jesus.

By now I was able to look back on some benchmarks he had given me for guidance. As He continually assured me, had I been wrong these bench marks happenings would not have occurred.

I knew that the wife, and I was doing everything within our power to follow Mt. 6:33

Well the end of the month was coming fast, and no rent for the back, or upcoming month.

11-99 Still just as broke as ever. This time I shook in my boots, as I made my way to the office to explain further that I had no rent money. This time she seemed more concerned, but gave a bit of encouragement saying that it would all work out. She enquired about the wife, and I, working, and I told her the conviction God had laid, on my heart. She didn't understand, but greatly respected me for my faith in God. So again she told me to stay in contact with her, and to keep her apprised of what was going on. I agreed. And so it continued for yet another month. By now it was Thanksgiving, and Christmas season, and the Lord enabled us to have a good Thanksgiving. But we lived with the constant fear, that some night we would come home, and our door would be padlocked. Despite the relentless pressure, and fear Satan put in our hearts we continued on with the work, God had called us to do, within the church. Surprisingly it kept our minds off of our problems.

I expected any day for a miracle to arrive. We kept praying, and believing for an answer.

The end of November arrived, and no back or current rent was in sight.

I knew that the third month we would be eligible for eviction, and I continued to bombarded, Heaven with that thought many times, "Trust Me! Men do what I will" He would respond. So we continued, but shaking in our boots.

Dec. 1, 99 I didn't even want to get out of bed. We had come to know, well the meaning of the song

Because HE Lives

1. God sent His Son, they call Him Jesus; He came to love, Heal, and forgive; He lived and died to buy my pardon, and empty grave is there to prove my Savior live.
2. How sweet to hold a new born baby, and feel the pride, and joy He gives; but greater still, the calm assurance, This child can face uncertain days because He lived.
3. And then one day I'll cross the river; I'll fight life's final war with pain; and then as death gives way to victory I'll see the lights of Glory and He lives.

Chorus—Because He lives, I can face tomorrow because! He lives all fear is gone; because I know He holds the future, and life is worth the living just because He lives.

For let me tell you, with problems of this nature, only God can help. One of the friends God put with us for this time of testing, made the statement; "Very few men purposefully try to avoid needed life expenditures such as rent. They would pay them if at all possible realizing the consequences if they don't." Having been in the Real Management business for years, no one more than me, realized this important concept. In fact I had locked out, and evicted many poor, well meaning individuals for far less rent then what I was behind, now I was faced with the same dilemma. Well despite my fear of eviction, I ambled over to the office, to advise the manager, that I still could not pay the rent. We exchanged usual pleasantries, and we found her to be very sympathetic. She inquired of the church helping us, and I replied that they were not aware of it. Again she asked about us going to work, and I again told her my feelings. She was concerned but said it would work out, and told us to stay in contact with her. I still continued to believe, that God would deliver us at any time. Yes we was willing to go this way, for at any one time, we could have walked away from it, got a job, but then, I had already been down that road, for I knew all too well the end of that way.

See Luke 17:33

Despite this dehumanizing debacle of rent being in limbo, The Lord provided for a good Christmas, but we still had this wet blanket, as it were hanging over our head. The wife and I spent hour after hour in prayer seeking God's face. The only solution to such nonsense is be not conformed. See Romans 12:2

Well the month came, and went, as usual, with no changes in our finances or rent. Approximately three days before the end of the year we were called to the office. With great fear, and trepidation, we slowly made our way to the office with our stomach in knots, thinking that perhaps this was it. But much to our surprise, when we got there Linda, The apt Manager was very sympathetic to our cause, and said: "she had decided to loan us the last three months rent as she didn't want her boss to force her to give us an eviction notice." WOW! What was it, that Jesus had beat in my head for the past months, "MEN DO WHAT I WILL" We couldn't believe it. She wanted me to sign a pay agreement, I refused saying that I would pay her if I could, but would not agree to any time table. She agreed, and then asked me about January's rent. I replied that it was same as the last three months. She stated that this would give us a little time to see what would happen. The wife and I went away from that office rejoicing with the load of eviction, and lock out being lifted.

ATTACKED ON EVERY FRONT

The rent was not the only problem. We seemingly were being attacked on every front, trying to get me to doubt God, and His faith covenant relationship. See ISAIAH 43:1-2

So far as I was concerned, the help from the manager was a properly timed bench mark. We seemingly were in-adamantly suspended between heaven and earth, capable of feeling the rain, the snow, the hail, the heat, even without the smell of smoke but none of it seemed to have any effect upon us. See Is. 43:1-2, Daniel 3:27

I kept reminding myself of what God had stated earlier (have at it see if you can trust me for fulltime ministry.)

2 Cor. 6:3-10, seemed to fit the trial to a T, right down to all areas of the proving time.

The lights, probably, was the worst of all to deal with primarily because the apartment we lived in, was total electric. And secondly the electric company had a zero tolerance for arrearage.

One time, (fortunate for us, it was warm weather), we had run the length of our extension, and was subject for a dis., connect. Following much prayer, the utilities head comptroller, gave me till Monday the following week, to pay the bill. Well Monday came, and still no money for which to pay the bill. When attempting to contact him, we learned of his vacation, and no one else could handle the bill, or grant a further extension. The thing was left in Limbo never knowing what to expect, but forcing me to be thankful each day for another day of electricity. When returning to his office on Wednesday, and finding the bill unpaid, and unable to contact me, he ordered a dis., connect.

Although we could have, we had never sought help, or assistance from anyone. We were living by faith, not a substitute for laziness, or a way to get out of work. We were working fulltime in ministry standing on the promise of God. I don't believe in obtaining help when one is capable of working.

In this particular instance, I wrote a check by faith (not recommended) having the lights turned on. I immediately went to The Disciple center and told them what had happened and they agreed to reimburse me for the check.

See Psalms 37:25

I will always believe God wanted me to feel the pain, degradation, and desperation, and hopelessness, with the lowest of humility of using government, or church sources as the case was asking for help.

They proceeded to ask me some of the most humiliating questions one could ask, and of course: "Why didn't I work?" It's hard to explain a question like that with: "I am living by faith."

For some strange reason when I played this thing to the end, I never had any further problems with paying it. Up until that time, I did not confess need, and I believe that after I had done all to stand then God took over.

SEE ARTICLE ON CONFESSING NEED

The phone, (used for the church van route), cable TV, (used for confirmations from ATB), all seemed to stay on, not without many test, and much prayer. Over and over suppliers would vow not to continue without payment in full but as the bills came due, the wife and I, would lay hands on them, and call the suppliers, and for some unknown reason (GOD) they would grant a continuance. Many of the bills were six, and seven months in arrears but they still stayed on.

God continually reminded me of what He had told me earlier, MEN DO WHAT I WILL. Time and time again I saw that promise come true.

TRANSPORTATION

We, had a car but no gas, and not enough money to buy plates. Limited transportation needs were meant through the church van. Fortunately we had a fairly wide area of coverage on the van route allowing us, to incorporate our necessary store running through it.

For fourteen months, we had no Money in our pockets to pay anything over and above the light bill and it was always in arrears.

Individuals were quick to give us food, and clothing, and our shoes seemed to last longer than usual. One individual had ordered two new suits and a number of slacks from, Haband, mail order house, and they accidentally sent him the wrong sizes, but he chose to give them to me as opposed to returning them.

God provided for our every necessity, and would always raise some one up, to help us out with the problem, but beyond specific, needs the general wants etc., one would like to have was, not a part of that list.

By now we were See gazing stock, see Hebrews 10:33

Year 2000

The new, year was well in progress, and still yet this thing continued to drag on with all the viciousness one could imagine. Rent was due again. One of the last things the apartment manager had said before we left her office that day of freedom was: "You ought to be able to stay ahead of the game." Well that sounded good, as no one (believe me) wanted too, more than the wife and I. But it obviously wasn't in the predetermined will of God.

Again I don't want to diminish God's care in any way for all of His promises are true, but from time to time it has been my experience that He chooses to withhold for a time for testing and proving.

I believe that this form of test has been proved over and over when looking to the book of Job, and the trials he went through. For reasons unknown, God chose to let the hedge down for a time, and I believe that's exactly what happened to me.

A prayer I had prayed many times after coming into the Gift of Pentecost, Lord I just wish that I could go out and find the biggest most expensive silver platter, I could afford, and with the necessary carving tools, my limited possessions, and my body, jump into your arms with the platter, and all attached giving Him the privilege to carve me any way He wanted. And I believe He done just exactly that. He replaced my cold stone dead heart with a new heart for the passion of God and His Kingdom.

Jan 2000 – March 2000 Well! What is the predetermined will of God? I must confess, I didn't know. The severe test continued on. Back nearly a year ago the pastor of New Beginning had prophesied to me, that God was going to put me in a box, and keep me there until He brought me to full and complete dependence upon Him, saying: "That there would be nothing I could do to get out of it, until He had achieved His purpose." So I always had that thought in the back part of my mind, and by now I really agreed with him.

But despite that, he kept encouraging me to go to work, and I kept telling him I could not do so, and stay within the confines of my conscience reference the Faith Covenant Relationship. He kept saying: "God would not tell me that." He still was not aware of any rent problems, nor for that matter any critical financial problems. Later he admitted to having thought that I had a retirement income. That was far from the truth, as I had exhausted my retirement savings months ago. We were living by faith.

But all of this did not appease the manager, who by now was getting upset, as I still was not able to pay any rent. As time marched on, she stated, she simply did not understand such a thing, nor had she known anyone with that type faith. I suppose one thing that always impressed her about me, was, I told her: "To evict me" but, she steadfastly refused, saying: "That wouldn't accomplish anything." She still was quiet concerned why the church wouldn't help me, and as I explained, I hadn't informed them about it. Matter of fact we felt it was a miracle that some of the debt load hadn't already become known, to the church but somehow it continued to be hid.

By the end of March, she stated: "That she had done all she could do to keep me from being evicted, and that more than likely, once she turned this thing in to the main office they would immediately move for an eviction:. We were, still believing that God would come through. But no answer was received.

I still had two computers, one lap top, and a desk top. God had provided miraculous for them. I used both of them in the ministry, and I sure didn't want to lose them. But as stated earlier monetary support, was not forth coming until I had liquidated everything of monetary value. I often thought of Dr. Roth's remarks he made when going through a particular trial: "I don't know what it takes to satisfy the demands of a Righteous God" well there is a lot of truth to that statement. And sure enough the call was coming for us to sell the laptop computer. Following much thought and prayer I pawned it, with the thought that I might be able to redeem it, at a later date, and still yet give me some living expense. But nothing, to pay for rent. A month later when the pawn shop fee came due on the lap top computer, I had no way to pay for it. In an effort to secure it I opted to pawn my desk top computer.

At that point, the wife was frantic, for she knew my love, and need for the computers. Just as frustrated, as I carried the computer downstairs to load in the car, I told her: "I will go to work, and redeem them both" and I well meant it.

Continuing downstairs, with computer in hand, The Holy Spirit whispered to me in perhaps one of the clearest voices I ever heard saying, "and you said you would play this thing to the end, yet you are going to jump boat on me, over the loss of a computer. Let me tell you that got my attention in a hurry. Within less than two or three days of that incident, Kent Pursell, came on TV preaching a sermon, the title: JUMPING THE BOAT. Well needless to say I lost both computers for I didn't go to work as Satan intended.

By now the storm clouds were gathering, and was brewing more than ever, and was soon to break.

Earlier we had started a discipleship class, and it was amazing at the way God Blessed. We had started out with the intentions of having a 10-12 week class and by now it had run close to a year with a good attendance.

It seemed to be, if you will, "a church within the church." Even the pastor was surprised of the interest continuing so long. There seemed to be no end in sight.

At about the same time our one year training/mentoring program had come to an end. The pastor seemingly was happy with our performance, and even took it upon himself to recommend us for a church. In the mean while, we continued our duties as assistant pastor. Still yet no mention was ever made of salary, and not wanting to express need, neither did I. From time to time various people would give us a few dollars and expressed concern as to why we were not getting a salary, but the pastor would always reply: "he couldn't afford one." Towards the end of April, he did finally tell the church that the Wednesday night offering would go to me, but still yet, that was never sufficient to cover my needs. There seemed to be some unfinished work in my life that God hadn't done.

At one point in time the pastor showed concern about the sparse offerings I received, but stated that if God wanted me to have more he certainly would have provided more. Well I felt there was a lot of truth to what he was saying so I continued on my faith walk, and continued with Mt. 6:33, knowing that God was making note of my involvements.

The firestorm of rent had not abated, but continued, more than ever. By now the manager, had notified the main office of my delinquency mid April, and so the main manager Jeanie wrote a letter advising me, that I had to the end of May to pay the rent in full, or they would evict me. The three months delinquency for the year 99 was not even mentioned by the house manager.

With much prayer, I contacted Jeanie and she was very firm, but polite stating: "That I needed to go get a job, and pay the rent on time." I told her the same as the house manager, that I couldn't work, and the reasons. I told her, I believed God would come through for me. She scoffed at the idea, but told me: "To remain in contact with her," so I did.

She reminded me, that there was no cheaper rent nowhere in this high dollar country $225.00 plus lights. Well having been in the rental business, I was well aware of that, and don't think for one minute, I didn't remind God of it. But as always, He would reply: "TRUST ME, I KNOW WHAT I AM DOING. MEN DO WHAT I WILL."

By now the end of May came, and still no rent. I called Jeanie having a nice talk with her, and without even asking, she said: "Well let's see what June holds." What had God beat into my head over and over? "MEN DO WHAT I WILL" I had already passed my termination point for my lease and she could have discontinued it at that point, but for some unknown reason (GOD) she didn't. Well June came and went still no rent.

PASTOR MADE AWARE BY ME OFFERING TO RESIGN

Near the end of June, I felt a real appetence, or urge to contact the pastor about resigning my job, or at the very least share with him some details reference my delinquent rent but because of expressing need. I used some hypothetical circumstances to tell him of our financial problems.

Not fully understanding the problem, he would not accept my resignation. But told me again, very emphatically, with much: insistences that I needed to get a job. He did not agree with my feelings, telling me God wouldn't tell me such a thing.

Miraculously my ordination had come through, and I had already been recommended by the pastor, and an evangelist friend of his, for a church, and had already received an invitation from a church to preach a trial sermon, before my rent problems, became known.

Not understanding any of this, I greatly feared for my licensing because of this debacle, but God had assured me, that He would secure them. So far as I was concerned, this amounted to another bench mark, of which God had been so faithful to give me.

With respect to the pastor, he was young enough to be my son, but despite that, I have always admired him, and was grateful to him for helping me to obtain my Pentecostal Ordination. But more than that, he seemed to be a mirrored image of me almost to the point of it being frightening, even to the point of the same business interest. He relentlessly and persistently pursued with zeal, his life's fleeting goals, even as much, if not more so then what I did, when I was his age.

And so it was with the rental business, he had established. In my tenure as assistant pastor, I had very few disagreements with him. If for some reason we couldn't agree on a given situation, we would disagree agreeably. But now, our harmonious relationship was about to be fractured, over an ever widening disagreement, on the ethics of work. For the record, let me state: "that I too am in favor of work, for I have well stated my feelings in the earlier part of this book, but when God has specifically ordered you to be involved with His ministry fulltime one had better take notice." I was not about to transgress, His request, for I knew all too well what happened in my earlier times.

As was the case, I was working fulltime in ministry.

Now came the news of this rent problem.

PASTOR MADE AWARE BY LANDLORD

The following day, the apartment manager, notified pastor, not with intent to hurt me, but to get me some help, (for she was still sympathetic to our need), in as much as the church wasn't paying the wife, and I, a salary.

PASTOR CALLED BOARD MEETING

The same night, without my knowledge, the Pastor called his advisory board, together for their advice. And on the same night, I had a nursing home service. When returning to the church, and learning of the meeting, I entered the meeting unaware as to the discussion in progress. I set on the board, but I was not asked to stay, likewise my son-in-law who had been with me for nursing home service, was not asked to stay.

They all acted strange, but were mum. I wondered why, but didn't give it much thought, till the following day, when I called the youth pastor, to inquire of the meeting. He side stepped the question, then called the pastor advising him of my phone call and interest. Within 30 minutes the pastor came to my residence, and advised me as to what the meeting was about reference the back rent, etc.

PASTOR GIVES ULTIMATUM

He gave me an ultimatum go to work, or else. He stated the church would not be responsible for my rent, and would not help me. He did not agree with me in any sense as to this faith walk, and was very irate, saying, I had sin in my life because I would not work. He gave me a few Bible verses scribbled on paper supporting his thoughts, of which I had went over many times, not to mention the many more, I knew about while seeking God's will.

But that seemed to be of no value, or interest to him. He was bent on me following his consciences, and not mine. He continually referred to his extra work activity, as sacrifice and praise for the cause of the ministry, but God's word says: "Obedience is better than sacrifice"

1 Sam. 15:22. I chose to continue in my own way, feeling that to do anything less would be paramount to not trusting and believing God, on my behalf. By now we had come through Hell and high water, and was not about to be deterred in any way, no matter what. And I believe God gave me a stronger resolve than ever to continue on in this stance.

Approximate time mid-July, the manager had given me till the end of July, but was poignant, short, and to the point about me catching the rent up.

In the mean time, I made a trip to Greston, Georgia, for a trial sermon. There were several ministers trying out for the pastoral position, so for near two weeks we waited for a reply.

THE DEVIL INCARNATE

Well by now, I was near to entering the point of no return, so far as staying at our apartment. I was attending a tent revival, and just about the time church started, a car looking exactly like my minister counselor friend's car pulled into the parking lot, looking as though he had been stuck in a red clay river bottom. The car was covered from top to bottom with red clay mud. So I left the tent, and walked across the parking lot to find out what had happened to his car.

Much to my surprise when getting to the area the car was parked in, there was a man setting on the curb tying his shoes. If I ever met the devil, I met him that night. His eyes glowed, and glared, literally penetrating my heart to the very core.

They seemed too protruded from his ashen colored face, on stems. His hair seemed to stand on end. He was ragged, and covered with mud, just like his car, and with the most hideous gut-wrenching grin, I ever saw, the words he uttered might nearly caused me to fall to the ground: "My first night homeless!" he declared. At that time, we seemed to be just a few weeks from being homeless ourselves. As I continued to talk to him, I started to lean on his car, and a attack dog from within the car tried to bite me. As it turned out, he had twelve attack dogs in that car. And I believed him. Moreover, if there was ever a devil incarnated man, it was him, sent directly from hell to further discourage me from carrying out the Masters orders. "TRUST ME."

THE WATER ROUGH BY NOW AT NEW BEGINNING

I well remember what John Johnson's mentor had told him one time. If it's of man it's bad, but if it's of the Devil it's wicked, but if it is of God it just doesn't make any sense.

Well that's what we all struggled with. Believe me, this entire rent thing, not to mention the loss of my integrity, and credibility for which they were not aware of, caused more frustration, and confusion, then one could imagine.

The pastor even accused me of causing confusion, Quoting, the following Bible verse, for reference. see 1 Corinthians 14:33

All I had to go by, was the bench marks, I believed God had been faithful to provide, along with numerous confirmations from ministry on ATB. By now wife and I were committed to play this thing to the end. We was not about to be deterred by a threat from the pastor, and yet we were well aware of our God given responsibility to our church elder, and pastor in the Lord. Did I not have a God ordained obligation to obey those that had the rule over me? That question weighed heavy on my mind. But somehow, I felt I had an overriding obligation to one higher than the pastor, and I stood my ground. I could not surrender my full faith and trust in God's provision to him or no one else. He asked me what my reasoning was for my stance, I quoted Mt. 6:33, and I was leaning heavy on Psalms 91

Because of my non compliance, with his request to go to work, he wanted my resignation, but chose perhaps, providentially, to table the matter until I could hear from the church.

He continued to openly oppose me to the board, saying: "God would not instruct me in such a manner."

Strangely enough, The Lord had revealed to me, that my ministry was about to start, but I didn't know what that meant.

Fortunately or unfortunately, I was asked to come back to Greston, Georgia for another trial sermon.

A TRIP WITH FEAR, AND A TEST ALL OF ITS OWN

On our first trip to Greston, Georgia approximately, 450 miles our son in law offered to drive us to the church, knowing that I didn't like to take an old car on long trips. On the way, he made a profound statement: "How could I trust God for a million dollar ministry, yet I couldn't trust him, with my old car on the road? Well I tried to ignore that statement all weekend but it hit something within my spirit that I couldn't explain. The following week Connie Moore stated on her TV. Show, "that FEAR IS NOT SIN SO LONG AS YOU DID'T LET IT ALTER YOUR COURSE." Wow! Well! I discounted both of them statements, but much to my surprise, within a week, I was asked to come back to Greston Georgia, for another trial service. Would I go? Again, I asked my son in law, but for one reason, or another he couldn't comply. So would I go, or not. I sure didn't want to, for I was fearful of the old vehicle I was driving. I had lost a car on the road one time, in earlier years, from overheating, and that's all I could see happening, causing us to be stranded, with no money, and no help. But God had different thoughts. So in response to my conscience, I consented to make that trip, in a car that had technically been totaled. I knew traffic would be heavy and the weather hot, so I shook in my boots, as we made our way toward Greston, Georgia. Sure enough, going through Atlanta, we came into a traffic jam unimaginable. As I suspected, the temperature gage begin to rise rapidly, bringing much fear to our hearts, but the wife, and I, laid hands on it, and said: "Lord I didn't want to come on this trip to begin with, driving this car, I only did so in obedience to you. So now you take care of the temp gauge for it's out of our hands." As I prayed that prayer, the gauge went down, to a safe operating level and stayed there for the rest of the trip. Following our sermon Sunday evening, we returned home, and the following day being so impressed with mechanical workings of the car, we made another 450 mile trip to Indiana to get our license renewed.

TURNED DOWN: AT GRESTON.

The week following my last visit to Greston, I was notified that I had not been accepted for
the pastorate of that church.

ASKED TO RESIGN

And on the following Wednesday 08-22-2000 following a lengthy board meeting I was asked to resign.

At one point previously the pastor had made two remarks that will always stick with me,

1. "Sometimes you have to be willing to look stupid for the cause of Christ."
2. "Sometimes you have to choose between ministry and God's Himself.

How could one separate himself from God's ministry? Well I didn't know, but I was about to find out.

I believe with all of my heart, I had to have, that choice. Would I choose God, and what He had so often verified to me, or did I choose his ministry and the church? Had I went to work, as the pastor ordered, I could have continued my tenure as assistant pastor. But I chose to obey God's word to me.

I was reminded of what the prophet had said earlier, in reference to having many chances to sell out.

RESIGNATION TIME

On Thursday, at our normal class time, I notified the discipleship class of my upcoming resignation the following Sunday. I informed the class that I no longer would be eligible to teach. The reason for resignation was not made known to the church, albeit one gentleman, a faithful attendee of discipleship class, and close friend, who had been brought into a closer relationship with Christ, and literally resurrected as it were, from a spiritual death, through the class, was much distraught, and continued to press me for the reason.

Being the close friend he was, I reluctantly shared with him a few details, trying not to express need. I told of my conviction to be in ministry only, and he empathized. He was disappointed to find out that I was not making a salary. Strangely enough he had been through similar circumstances, and even now was facing a life and death struggle with a brain tumor. Likewise the wife and I were facing a life and death struggle through the possibility of being homeless.

SUNDAY NIGHT the pastor insisted that I go before the church, and give a resignation speech, and so in compliance with his request, I did, as he requested. I used very vague terms, as I really did not know any more than anyone else, why this was all happening. I gave the quote from John Johnson's mentor, (quoted earlier), and concluded the speech with all of the usual condolences and turned it over to the pastor who likewise gave his condolences. That ended a chapter in my life, which I will never forget. But despite the problems at hand, I felt a calmness and serenity of peace as I had never known. Angels were baring me up in their arms just as the scripture says.

I loved that job, and appreciated the pastor for his help, and would not have done anything to jeopardize it in any manner, I regretted having to take this course of action, but felt I had no choice.

Following church, our friend and his wife (from discipleship class) invited us to their house for supper, and then gave me a check for two months rent 450.00. To God: be the glory. This was just in time to pay the Aug. rent. Management stated: "that if I would continue to pay two month's rent each time, until the back rent was paid that I could stay."

FIRST DAY OF MY NEW MINISTRY

Following that fateful night, The Lord reminded me, that the first night of my own ministry had started. I still had no understanding of this. The pastor had informed me, that since I held International Holiness, license, I would have to attend a CH church. Unfortunately there was no other CH church within driving distance. And so for the next several months, I floated between churches, always making sure that I at least attended the CH church I had just got booted out of, once or twice a month, to stay within the requirements of my licenses.

THE BLACK SHEEP OF THE CHURCH

After all of the happenings, the wife, and I was the black sheep of the bunch. Word had gotten out, that I wouldn't work, and that I wouldn't support my wife, and who knows what else was being told. All Hell seemed to be against us. Faced with so much opposition, and not being allowed to participate, we seldom attended that church as they all seemed to just give us the cold shoulder.

TWO FAMILIES BY OUR SIDE
GOD ORDAINED

God had ordained to families to be with us in this time of testing, the one gentlemen who earlier I had mentioned from discipleship class, and one lay minister and counseling professor, and my senior by several years, who had attended the church, off and on, for about the same period of time as wife, and I.

I had shared with him limited information, about some of the circumstances we were going through but at the same time trying to refrain from expressing need. I know that he spent many hours in prayer for guidance, reference these trying times. Many times, He stood by me as God provided. Likewise he had a full time call to the ministry and was prohibited from working secular jobs.

THE DEVIL SAID, "NOW WHO WILL PAY YOUR RENT?"

Shortly after the gentleman from discipleship class, had given us the rent money, he was admitted to the hospital, the second time, for removal of a brain tumor. And the devil said so plainly: "Now who will pay your rent?"

RESTRICTIONS PLACED ON US IN MINISTRY

One of the restrictions we had placed on us by the pastor, and board at time of resignation, was that we could not minister to any New Beginning people albeit the gentleman from (discipleship class) was so frustrated with the church board and pastor for not helping us, that he, and his wife chose to break off his relationship, with the church. Likewise because of the incident, the pastor, and church seem to forsake both families, who were standing with us in this critical issue.

Because of the church neglecting these two families, I continued to fellowship, and pastor them when needed.

From about August thru November we made regular trips back and forth to the hospital some thirty five miles one way to maintain regular visit, and to stand with them in their hour of need.

The church they supported since its beginning now had all but forsaken them. Here this man was in the hospital, flat of his back, unable to work, with no income, likewise the wife, was unable to work do to sickness (no income) yet they still continued to pay our way back and forth, because they just needed someone. We later learned that they were living on credit cards, even borrowing on one, to pay for another. That is a dreadful way to live.

Yet they couldn't look for help from the church, whom they supported all those previous years.

OUR RENT PROBLEMS CONTINUED

By now, it was September and our rent was due again, if you recall correctly we had paid two months, the previous month, but management wanted to hold the second month to pay for arrearage. Management was not the least bit happy to find out that we were unable to pay the rent due. Howbeit they gave us to October 1.

OUR LAST WARNING
AND TIME OF NO RETURN

Well time was swiftly passing, and I still was working in accordance with Matt. 6:33. I had already tried and proven it, and I knew that somehow it would work. Still yet, my rent was unpaid, and by now we had reduced our household holdings, to a TV (used for confirmation), and non sellable items i.e., a couch, bed, and a microwave oven, with some various misc. The management kept stressing, over and over, that we would never find anything cheaper to rent, in all of Pearl County. This is a point, that I continued to tell God over and over, but all I could get in response was TRUST ME! I KNOW WHAT I AM DOING.

Well by now they had terminated the lease, and I was past the point of no return. Up until now I could have went to work somewhere and paid the monthly rent, but now my time was gone. Did I not have an obligation to my wife, to keep a roof over her head? What obligation did I have to the Lord vs. my wife? Seemingly the more I questioned His Divine Orders, the more confused I became myself. They did not make sense, yet I felt as though I was locked into this thing, to the finish. These were arguments that I tried over and over to reconcile, but finally just ended up doing as God told me to do.

By now November was here, and time was swiftly moving ahead. The management by now was pressing me to move. I cried, night and day to the Lord, but seemingly with the same words, TRUST ME, I KNOW WHAT I AM DOING.

Just about the time, I had decided to move (no money) James Delbar came on TV., one day, and was talking about some sought of a struggle he was having, in which his wife, was pressing him to make a decision. He said to her, as he stated on TV, "If God don't care, why should I." That settled the question for me.

For the past 14 months, I had never had more then 10-15 dollars in my possession at one time, beyond my various needs which seemed to not be my rent. And this was the case now.

Consequently we was unable to move, so we stood still telling, The Lord our problems. It would have been very easy to let our needs be known, but our hope was in The Lord, not men.

On the fifteenth of November the manager advised that they had filed an eviction suit. Shortly after, we received the summons, from the court to appear Nov. 30, 2000. The first time in all of my life I had ever been evicted. Despite the continued rent problems, and still not expressing our need to anyone, we still continued our ministry, to the two couples, The Lord had put within our care. From talking with an attorney, I found out, that they probably would give us three to ten days, to move once we appeared before the judge.

Still, we didn't say a word to no one.

We had hoped that no one, we knew would be at the court proceedings, to hear what was happening.

On the day, we was ordered to appear, the sister of the gentlemen from discipleship class, whom we had ministered too, routinely, in the hospital, was at court, with her daughter for an unknown reason. They had an earlier date, to appear, but it had been postponed to the same date we were scheduled.

That was most unfortunate for us, because here I was, a minister, and having ministered to her family was being evicted for none payment of rent, but we had no control over that.

It appears God had providentially placed her there for this hour of need.

Appearing before The Judge, he stated: "You have ten days, to move, after which if you are not out, we will move you out."

I recall, as I turned from the judge, (after having heard the verdict) seeing her, and she had sought of a sick grin on her face, and I nodded, and left.

Did I ever feel stupid, humiliated, and low down, for allowing my wife to be put thru the whole ordeal Luke 14:26

I knew all too well what that meant for as I stated earlier, I had used the courts many times, to do the same thing, with little, or no sympathy, for any one, in my management job. One would ask, why I went this far. Believe me! I wanted to comply with management, in the worst way, but it seemed to beyond my control, at least to stay within the faith covenant relationship, that God had moved me into, and the wife whole heartedly agreed.

That never forgotten court date was on Thursday November 30, 2000, and in as much as December 10 fell on Sunday the court clerk said I could stay in the apartment till Monday December 11. Believe me that was the furthest thing from my mind. But I had no place to go, and for all I knew at that time, I would be living in the car, and as it was the case, the tank was setting on empty. Satan had told me many times that I would be homeless, and now it appeared, as if he was correct.

The entire thing was beyond my control, as I had no alternate choice, but to move.

But for now we chose to stay there, and play it to the end.

The next Sunday, December 3, we attended church at the place where we were the black sheep of the bunch, and the pastor approached me, and said: "You are going to be forced to move this next week, aren't you" (I was unsure, as to how he knew.),

I said in return: "It appears so, but we will see." I said:

"Jefferson, you know what you said earlier "Sometimes you have to be willing to look stupid for the cause of Christ,"

He interrupted, saying: "You sure have done that ok." I said:

"Jefferson, I would hate to stand before my God knowing that I didn't do all to please Him:

I said: "I have done that, and now it is in His hands. I have no regrets. I don't know what will happen but in the final analysis, He will rule."

Muttering, he said: "I am just glad that I am out of it, you do what you want," and he walked away.

By now Satan made the wife and I, feel as if we had a death sentence hanging over our head.

71

But we stilled stood on the promises of God, knowing what, He had done earlier, and knowing the constant revelations he had spoken to me. TRUST ME! I KNOW WHAT I AM DOING. He reminded me of my commitment of FAITH, LOVE, AND OBEDIENCE, WRAPPED, IN A GARMENT OF PRAISE.

That's the key. Throughout the Old Testament many battles were won by using this technique, and no more. That's what we were determined to do.

By now time was dwindling down, and by now it was Tuesday, and we still didn't know what we would do. Gloom, and doom hung over our heads as if to be a heavy storm cloud about ready to burst forth its ravaging effects upon earth, but we kept praying and seeking Gods face. We literally felt the Angels whizzing by, sounding like small jets doing battle, over and over, for the duration of the time we were at this location, Confirmed by our minister, and counselor friend.

On Tuesday, our friend from discipleship class, by now partially paralyzed, because of the brain tumor, being removed, and unable to drive, ask us to take them on some errands. Their first stop was the bank, for which they had some unattended business to wrap up, due to an inheritance, they had recently received. Much to our surprise at the conclusion of their business they called us to the desk, and handed us a check for $2500.00 See Ecclesiastes 10:19

No truer words were ever spoken. Wife and I sure had a celebration that night. SIX DAYS before being homeless, we came into this money. Now then we had a way to proceed. Up until that time, we had no idea what we might have to do. I spent many nights wondering just how this thing would play out, for the devil was quick to tell me that I was wrong, not to mention the sharp rebukes about sin in my life that I had received from the pastor, and his associates who maintained all along, I was wrong. I think every Imp in Hell, was playing this thing for all it was worth. But now they had been proven wrong. Had I been wrong I would have been homeless, and destitute with no place to go, and no money in my pocket, but that was far from the case.

The next few days, was a breeze, considering what we had just went through, but still we had concern of just where we might go, for not too many people will rent to one who has been evicted, not to mention what the landlord had said earlier, that our rent was the cheapest place in all of Pearl County. And I couldn't have agreed more. With our credibility, and integrity, at an all time low, how would we ever find a place any cheaper no possible way.

By Saturday, I had vowed to be out of this place, but when the wife, and I woke up, she ask me: "Well what are we going to do?"

I said: "The Lord says wait." So against our so called better judgment, we decided, that we would play it right down to the last day that we was to be out. The first thing Monday morning, I called the office, to see if they would let me pay another two months, rent, but as stated earlier, we had crossed the point of no return.

We had some concern, but who worries with $2500.00 in your pocket. I rented a u-haul van, and loaded our meager possession, in it, and prepared to move them to storage.

The daughter, not fully understanding any of this, and being upset, with the church, over the whole ordeal, offered to let us move in with them. Matter of fact, they begged us to move in with them, for her husband was in truck driving school, at the time and they were short on pay.

Wife, and I, opted to take her up on the offer, consequently being able to help them, as much as it helped us. We had planned to stay in a motel until suitable arrangements could be made.

ANOTHER BENCHMARK

Another bench mark. We had no sooner got our belongings loaded then the song, IT IS FINISHED, incessantly came to mind. Three thousand songs, perhaps one knows, and yet the song of all songs, begin to play over and over in my mind.

THE SONG IT IS FINISHED
1. There's a line that has been drawn thru the ages, on that line stands The Old Rugged Cross, and on that cross the battle is raging, for the gain of man's soul or his loss.
2. On one side stands, the forces of evil, all demons, and devils of Hell, on

the other side, The Angels of Glory, and they meet on Golgotha' Hill,

3. The earth shakes with the forces, of the conflict, the sun refuses to shine, for their hangs Gods' Son in the balance, and then thru the darkest He cries

4. Yet in my heart the battle was raging, not all the prisoners of war have come home, they were battle fields of my own making, they did not know that the war had been won.

5. Then I hear that The King of Ages has fought all of my battles, for me, and victory was mine for the claiming, and now praise His name I am free.

Chorus It' is finished, the battle is over, it is finished, there will be no more war, It is finished the end of the conflict, and it is finished and Jesus is Lord.

ANOTHER BENCHMARK

Another bench mark. This was now Dec. 11, and we had not paid a cable bill for might near 7mos.

When I would call, the finance lady would just respond with: "Well do what you can" and the cable stayed on. The last two of them 7mos, I didn't even bother to call them, because I didn't know what to tell them, but the cable stayed on. Why? I believe because, I had received confirmation after confirmation on ATB of which we watched practically all the time. In fact after such a rough time at the church it turned out to be our church. We owed well in the excess of $250.00 but it stayed on.

In an effort to save miles and gas, we left the u haul truck parked at the apartment complex overnight by managements permission, enabling, us to drive the car to our daughter's house. The next day, we returned to the apartment complex to pick up the truck, and there was a note, from cable Company, on the door saying, they were going to disconnect the cable. Now that is funny, for it had stayed on all that time but the day after we moved out they shut it off, and I never told them.

THE HOUSE OF OBED EDOM

This is what our minister friend said: the Lord whispered to him, saying that: we were temporarily living in the house of Obed Edom. Well we had a nice Christmas spending it with the four grandbabies and parents. Matter of fact, it had just been three years before, that we had done the same thing spending, Thanksgiving, through Christmas, with them under much better circumstances. For we, were on a visit from Indiana.

Following these events, I spent many nights, with mixed emotions, trying to reconcile within my mind, reference Human logic vs. Divine logic. I simply didn't understand. No one understood it. No one would accept it, but our two special friends, God had put with us. Where did my responsibility lie? Was it with God, or was it with my wife, and creditors.

The end of the year was approaching fast, and the New Year 2001 was looming on the horizon. A few nights before the new year, the wife and I visited James Moran's church to hear a prophetess Betty Gibson speak, That night Miss Gibson spoke a word of prophecy over the wife, saying that she was going to get a miracle right at the first of the year.

And for months on end, The Lord by revelation to me, continually referred to an incident that had happened about three years earlier, in the daughters back yard, reference a swimming pool. He further stated, that the incident that I had observed with that pool, would be mild in comparison with what would happen reference the soon to be miracle. Even more interesting, he told me, that it would happen less than one hundred yards from where the original incident took place. Well I didn't know anything about it, I just believed.

The incident centered, around a large circler swimming pool in the back yard which had sprung a leak. After several days of trying to get the water out with no success, (and the wife setting on the down side of the pool in a plastic lawn chair), I just happened to push down the liner a bit under the level of water and the entire contents of the pool emptied out with a loud swish in just a matter of a few seconds, washing everything within its path away. With just a bit more power, it would have washed the plastic lawn chair right out from under the wife, for it indeed did shake and move it. Comical: to say the least.

Well it happened Thursday night, before New Years, the following Monday. I was a sleep, less than one hundred yards from where the pool incident had occurred, and I remember seeing Jesus, as it were on a sea of glass out several hundred feet. The last I recall, I saw Jesus, raising His arms. At first a speckled dove flew in a circle around me, and landed on the ground at my feet, nibbling on some grain. And then the thunder started to crash, and the lightning began to flash, and the wind began to fiercely blow. As I looked up, the roof begin to separate from the walls, exposing the interior of the walls, and with that, the wiring begin to spark, and the next thing I knew, I begin to see the lightning flash in the sky.

As I looked up again, I observed a large swell of water coming at me, over the wall. It was similar to what you see in a hurricane on television. With that I buried my head in the pillar expecting to be washed away, at any time, and the wife came in, and Asked, What's happening?

I said: "I am about to get washed away." Well it was all a dream.

Now came Sunday, and the comptroller over the housing authority, for housing in this area, contacted me, in church, and told me, to go see the office girl the first thing Tuesday morning the day after New Years. This man had had a few ties with the church, and we had been rather reluctant to see him. Our friend's sister who had observed the court proceedings, was employed by this man, indicated his willingness, to help us. Fortunately he did not listen to all of the rumors that were circulating. A few days before, we had already picked up a application, from the management of this complex, but everything the application called for, we was unable to answer truthfully, so we just left it blank.

Acting upon his request, we approached the office girl on Tuesday. As I started to hand her the blank application, I said: "Rita" I don't know what you know about our circumstances these last 14 months but we haven't paid any rent the whole time," (and she burst out crying) surely, she said, "it must have been of the Lord, because they are under the same rules we are, and we couldn't let you get by for more than a month, without filing for an eviction."

She reviewed, the blank application, marking whatever she wanted and said: When do you want your apartment? She had told us earlier, when we first approached her about an apartment, that she didn't expect to have one for three or four months.

I said: "whenever you have one," not expecting to have one for at least 2 months.

She says: "well it will be $50.00 plus a deposit."

The wife, and I, both surprised by now, blurted out; "You mean you have one."

She says: "Yes, and you can move in it today."

Well the devil got caught in another lie. Now we had an apartment six times cheaper, then before, and no utilities. I questioned her about having a satellite dish, in as much, as I knew, I owed a large cable bill, but she said we couldn't have a dish on the premises, so hopes of receiving our beloved ATB was dashed.

Well like always The Lord had the final say so. After getting our few meager possessions moved in, The Lord, again, completely furnished the apartment to the fullest. We moved in on Tuesday, and Wednesday, the same week, and on Friday, we happened by the cable office, and I told the wife, I am going to pay them a visit and see if I could work something out with them so we can get Cable TV.

When approaching the clerk, I ask her, how much I owed, and expecting to hear the amount previously stated, I was shocked to hear that I only owed $21.00, someone, she said had paid for me as a Christmas Present. No one knew but the Lord Jesus. So you tell me.

LIFE IN OUR NEW RESIDENCE: AT APPLE LANE PEARL CITY, TENNESSEE

01-02-01 to 11-17-2002

One of the many promises to me, by revelation, was that we would stand before all men owing no man nothing, but love, and that every creditor I ever had since of legal age would be opened to me, albeit I wouldn't need it, strangely enough confirmed by a vision.

I alluded earlier in the fore part of this (book), of how we were forced into bankruptcy. One of my many questions to The Lord when He called me into ministry, was how could I stand before people owing them money? Not only had I filed bankruptcy and had partially rebuilt my credit, but when having entered into this faith walk, I lost all integrity, and credibility. To date my bills had not been canceled, but still remained in limbo. Believe me, every creditor that I have, is a testimony, to the power of God, and, to the fact, that I am on the right track. For: I should have been in court a thousand times, but beyond court, for the rental proceedings, that hasn't occurred.

This fact was no more in evidence, then when our disabled friend's daughter, applied for an apt at the same complex we were living at, shortly after we moved in, and she was turned down because of credit problems. Her credit was snow white compared to ours.

Having asked our friend about the situation, he said, and I quote: "We both know why you got in the apt" referring to God's help. Only God could have bridged that gap. He looks out for the ones who trust Him.

Well for the next few months things seem to progress slowly but with many blessings. We continued our ministry with the two couples the Lord had put with us.

The disabled man and his wife, and the counselor minister friend and his wife.

On Sunday we would have church at the apt. both morning and night, with whom, ever the Lord sent in, and on Wednesday we would have Bible study at our disabled friends, house. (They were unable to attend our Sunday Services at our house) because of his disability.

In addition to this, two to three times per week we would assist our disabled friend, in getting to their various appointments, as neither he, nor his wife could drive.

In addition, we were still involved more or less as the assistant chaplain for the local county jail.

BACK TO THE SWEAT BOX

In late fall, following our friends recovering from surgery, the Lord told me to go back to New Beginning fulltime, confirming it through three of the most unlikely individuals. We had no doubts of God's command, and felt we had no choice but to comply, and so we returned, but it was not without much opposition.

We were unable to participate in anything, as the people treated us like dirt.

The wife, and I, was always active in Sunday school, discussion, but it seemed as though they were disgruntled even if we participated in that. So we sat. For some unknown reason, I seemed to be under mandate to go to every service, even during a tent revival. Up until now, I had preached at every tent revival sponsored by the church, since being connected with the church, but now it was a no, no, for I had sin in my life. (So they thought!)

Following three weeks of attendance, a friend from across the street from our residence, James, who had attended our church on occasion came to me, very troubled reference their home church that He and his family had been attending. The church had all but shut down, with little or no functions left. He was highly concerned for his married children who likewise attended the church.

In the process of time, and with much prayer, God released me from New Beginning, leading me to reinstate our church in the house, and to Name it, The New Hope. In addition we felt lead, to invite those, who now had no church home, as result of the split.

The following Sunday, we had sixteen people attending our church, in the house. The following Sunday, they had dwindled down to eleven, and then the split church, reorganized, leaving us again with just two, to six attendees.

Well that seemed to be our stance for the time being.

As I mentioned earlier, in order for me to keep my ministry credentials, I had to be actively involved with a church of my denomination, or else be involved with full time evangelism. I had registered The New hope with the district presbytery, which provided me a covering for my credentials, as well as, much needed experience in many other areas.

Shortly after the registration of the church, it began to gravitate, to deep Theological discussions that literally forced me, to dig deeper then I had ever before. Over the next few months, wife and I, would dig into depths of the Bible that we didn't know existed. The Lord reminded me, that we was doing exactly the same as several of the Biblical talk show host, only they had a camera trained on them, and we didn't.

From time to time, we was privileged to have one or two neighbors come to our services, in which case we would have a normal service, but for the most part it was the original three couples.

REST AND PEACE UNLIKE EVER BEFORE

As of June 2001, our rent was only $50.00 monthly, our utilities free, with cost for overages only, and due to a mistake on our cell phone bill, we had six months of free service passed on to us. In addition we was privileged to tour this area in (servant hood) transportation, of our disabled friends, and with that we was eating in the finest of restaurants, probably more than at any other time in our life.

With no other current bills, and everything else in limbo, this gave us a sense of freedom and peace that we hadn't known for months. I remember just wanting to sleep, but my brute instinct, would not let me. I remember the Lord telling me to just relax, and enjoy myself (His Will Always). Little by little the wife and I did, but had we known what lay ahead, I can assure you, that I would have heeded the Lord's command, more earnestly.

Well ministry to the two couples continued through November 2001, almost a year to the date, that I had begun this venture. The following month I came down with strep throat, so the wife continued with it by herself.

By this time the counselor, and minister friend and his wife who had been with us from the beginning of this walk, now begin to feel a call elsewhere and rarely attended. Likewise I begin to feel my call being discontinued with the servant hood ministry.

From the time of expiration of our ministry with New Beginning in Aug. the Moran's had been very helpful to us in every manner. It seemed as though the Lord gave us favor with them in every manner.

Not only had they given us the $2500.00 initially, but they continued to support us with their tithe money, and in addition purchased our groceries, and other needful items. Not to mention the gifts they continued to buy for the wife, (seemingly a union made in Heaven). Bro. Moran a minister in the beginning had given up as a minister, because of innuendo being circulated about He, and his first wife. Matter of fact, as I alluded to earlier, it seemed as though God, had ear marked his ministry to be similar as mine, not seeking secular employment, ministering to the poor and homeless, being put right in the midst of a bunch of secular, high societal parishioners with a penchant for material needs far to exceed any Biblical standards. The pressure was too much, and he literally gave up, and became rather bitter. Seemingly the disciple class that I alluded to earlier in the first part of this book renewed his dead spirit.

ALBEIT LATE NOVEMBER, THE FAVOR THAT HAD BEEN SHOWED US EARLIER, BEGAN TO DECLINE

One of the first issues that became apparent was a matter about faith. Based on Bro. Moran's remarks, apparently in the earlier part of his ministry, he was living by faith even as we were, but now being disgruntled with ministry, his faith level seem to plummet to ground zero. Every time I mentioned anything reference Gods' promises to me, reference my faith walk, he would always counter it with "Well that's how I always believed, but nothing ever happen it was just a false belief. When continually being bombarded with this type doubt, one has a tendency to start doubting himself. No doubt in my mind, he and his wife, was affecting our faith level. It was later revealed to me by the Lord, and confirmed through my minister counselor friend, that the door was shut because of this problem.

Another issue that came to the front was food stamps. Mid-November they made the suggestion that the wife and I should apply for food stamps. I declined, saying that: "I simply felt, that if I had to start depending on food stamps, as opposed to God, then it was time for me to go to work." They immediately ceased buying groceries for us.

The servant hood ministry that we, were providing them with seem, to gravitate more and more to employment then ministry.

In the beginning they would always check to see if my schedule coincided with their plans, but now they seem to make their own plans and expected the wife, and I, to conform to their schedule, with little or no concern for our schedules, always with the threat that they could get someone else to do the task, whatever that might be, if for some reason we couldn't comply.

Strangely enough, about two weeks before everything started falling apart, our counselor minister friend's wife, made a statement in the presence of our disabled friends, stating: "That we ought to start attending their church since at present, I was ministering to the wife, and the wife was ministering to me only. I stated very plainly, the conviction that I had an obligation to The Lord to maintain normal church hours on Sunday, and Wednesdays, as The Lord had entrusted me with. I further indicated, that I would continue in this walk, until being released from this given assignment.

CHRISTMAS TIME AGAIN

Well by now it was Christmas time. Our income had dwindled to $140.00 per month, and no groceries. With rent, and groceries, gas, etc. there was no money left over for any Christmas. Ever since we had been in this faith covenant relationship, our adverse finances seem to abate near the Christmas season, allowing us to have a nice Christmas. We had no reason to think any different about this Christmas, but now it seemed to be different. All doors were shut, reference getting any gifts, either for the wife or me, but more importantly the children, and Grandbabies. As I had mentioned earlier we were living by faith, with a command not to be involved with secular employment. We to date, had always stayed within the bounds of this Covenant Relationship, and did not want to break it. Our needs were being met, but our wants, in this instance, did not seem to meet the criteria for being answered. So we had two options, violate the faith covenant agreement, and go get a temporary job, or forget about buying Gifts for our special ones.

Perhaps this was one of the toughest decisions we ever had to make. What would we tell the children, and especially the grand children?

When one is involved with this type of relationship with The Lord Jesus one does not want to break it at any cost. Luke 14:26 Luke 14:33

The wife and I made the small trek to our daughter's house, Christmas Day, for a dinner, and normally what was a gift exchange. When time came to exchange gifts, we gathered the grandbabies around (with The Lord very much in control), and refreshed their memories, reference, their dad's recent driving school, in which they had endured some hard times. As we told them that day, that mama, and papa was in a school of sorts (literally a school of divine origin) reference ministry, and as result we just didn't have any money for which to purchase gifts at this time. Following this revelation, we had prayer, and ate dinner, and returned home glad that we didn't bow, or sell out to mortal man once again.

There again everything of value in this life cost something, and the price for ministry is no different, no matter what happens it is cheap at any cost.

MORE DECISIONS

As I mentioned earlier our contact with the Moran's, had been somewhat limited nearly 30 days, first by my strep throat, and now my wife's illness. For I no sooner got well then she became ill.

In addition, we were trying to be careful not to cause an infectious situation with Mr. Moran because of his recent and serious surgery, knowing that his immune system was weakened. The family had expressed their paranoia many times, over this type thing, and rightfully so. On two occasions, with his health in mind, we canceled our appointment with them, to take him to the doctor. This further exasperated the ever widening gap between us. Finally the straw that broke the camel's back was in January 2002, The Moran's ask me to dismiss prayer meeting, and take them to a financial planning seminar with promise of a free meal at an elite restaurant. Earlier they had heard my response to my minister friend, about attending their church as opposed to keeping intact our own services in our house, and now they were demanding that we dismiss services for this dinner meeting. I steadfastly refused.

I reiterated, the need to maintain my church hours, as God had directed us to do. As result they discontinued their support of us. Probably God ordained, for the above mentioned reasons, and a test to see if I could be controlled by finance.

At time of coming into this testing time, our order, for the walk, The Faith Covenant

OBEDIENCE UNTO DEATH, THRU THE FOLLOWING COMMANDS

1. The command not to seek secular employment was still in force.

2. Do not sell anything to raise funds, as God was ready to return everything, back to me I lost.

3. Do not confess need.

Well Feb. 2002 came in, with no support. Where would we go from here?

We begin to have rental problems again with no income. We had already been down this road once, and felt very much that we would no longer be faced with such a problem. The Lord had been so merciful to us the last year supplying our rent, and utilities' now then we again faced the prospect of delinquency. We knew all too well what had happened before, and Satan was sure not to let us forget.

THE COMMAND FOR A HIGHER LEVEL OF FAITH

First to middle of March the Lord by revelation stated, and I quote" I desire for you to go on into the Land beyond limits. Presently you are at the land of more than enough.

I said: "Lord, I am tired. Speaking rather reluctantly I stated: "I still have not achieved the goals that I, wanted in ministry, I would just like to get on with this ministry.

He stated, "But I desire for you to go on to a higher level of faith and trust in me." (In other words get out of the boat and walk with me in deep water)

His voice was rather passionate, and intense, and with that tone of voice and His magnetic pull, only Jesus can have, I said: "Ok Lord have it your way. He then reminded me of His Words. (Luke 5:3-6)

On that day, on the shores of, the Sea of Galilee, Peter responded in desperation as I did, but you know the end of the story. He later revealed that had I insisted on having it my way, I would never have reached the Land beyond limits, and most likely would have only a small ministry the rest of my life, if at all.

He stated: "That I my age, He didn't want me to have to worry about finances etc. as most ministries did, and by going through this extra proving time I would not have too."

Almost immediately my life began to fall apart, and self destruct, in every respect.

See Gal. 2:20

Incommunicado seem to be the order of the time.

A prisoner of our own circumstances, yet free to make a choice of continuing this walk, or to walk away from it.

Yes at any time we could have liquidated what few remaining assets we had, and then opted to get a job, but the wife and I, felt that would have only worsened the problem, but more importantly the loving relationship that we had developed between us, and The Lord Jesus, was so overwhelming, to us. How could we fail Him?

At one time in particular I seriously had negotiated with a dealer about liquidating a few pins, and trophy that I had left, and indeed had accepted the thirty five dollars, and in the process, God literally screamed at me: What are you doing? I became so rattled that I gave the dealer back his money and forgot about the sale.

When one is going through this type problem, inevitably one looks for a way of escape, but The Lord Jesus reminded me, many times that He could have walked away from the cross and His Father's will, but He chose to go this way, in order that we might have life.

Opposition did not cease, for all concerned, thought we were looney tunes, and elcrazos, including our family.

Strangely the more we entered into this additional proving time, the visions became more prevalent, and frequent, then ever. Seemingly everything that I had received in revelations, reference the ministry, was now being given to me by visions.

Almost as though a television was playing before my vary eyes.

In times past, while being at the former apt complex, I along with my mentor friend heard the whizzing of angels round about, but now visible Angelic visitation was all about me, not to mention the multiple visions of The Lord Jesus.

Unlike before, I was unable to keep my cable, allowing me to see ATB. The individual, within the cable company, who was most helpful to me earlier, was unable to help us out this time as her boss over-rode her consent to continue our cable. This occurred several different times. Finally it was shut off permanently. Again we could have sold some of our furnishing for a short duration of continuance, but we could not do so because of the covenant.

Likewise, I was unable to keep the cell phone. Over and over, I had negotiated with the cell phone provider for extension, but now that too seem to come to a grinding halt, and we was without any form of communications.

REMAINING MINISTRY CAME TO A GRINDING HALT

The loss of the Jail ministry was defiantly a blow, as I always enjoyed preaching to the inmates. But now the jail chaplain advised that the facility was being shut down to all ministry' until the new jail construction was completed. That was a whole year away.

Item #2 of the faith-covenant, relationship (not to sell anything to raise money became a force that I would have to reckon with many times.

At about the same time all of this was happening, The Lord coined the phrase TWICE DEAD PLUCKED UP BY THE ROOTS, to illustrate what was happening to us, not necessarily applicable to Jude 1:2. Well I didn't know what this all meant but I was beginning to find out.

Just a short time before my tenure ended, at New Beginning Worship I had preach a sermon on John 12:24 but if you die. Well I was experiencing death, in a way, that I had never known, being dead to all.

THE SONG ROCK OF AGES CLEFT FOR ME!

1. Rock of Ages cleft for me Let me hide myself in Thee, Let the water and the blood, from Thy wounded side which flowed, be of sin the double cure, saved from wrath, and make me pure.

2. Could my tears forever flow, Could my zeal no longer know, These for sin could not atone, Thou must save and Thou alone, In my hand no price I bring, simply to Thy cross I cling.

3. While I draw this fleeting breath, When my eyes shall close in death, When I rise to worlds unknown, and behold Thee on Thy throne, Rock of Ages cleft for me, let me hide myself in Thee.

By now, our rent was beginning to run in serious delinquency. Our rent was only $50.00 per month which again, could have been paid by liquidating assets, but at least for the time being that seem to be out of the question. Our utilities was routinely paid for, by the housing authority and the only thing that we was charged for, was overage, plus any late charges. Well by now we, had amassed a total bill of $109.00, consisting of $20.00 overage on utilities and late charges, At, $10.00 per month accrued.

Eagerly seeking some way to circumvent an eviction, looming on the horizon, I begin to poor over the rental contract. When doing so, The Lord seemed to highlight a section, that seem to indicate, that if one was paying a minimum rent, as I was, one could apply for hardship, and with their permission, would be granted a waiver, of paying rent. When approaching management about this clause, they was not sure of its meaning, but when checking with housing officials, they confirmed the meaning, as I had stated, and granted me a waiver, of rent, but not utilities. The no rent policy was in effect for the next ten months. Well God was in control.

Loss of car

Satan had already told me that we were going to lose our car, and that we would be walking out of the complex, with just the clothes on our back. That's a frightening thought. God had to continually give me more grace than ever to deal with the upcoming problem. The prospect of what Satan had told me, seem to loom more and more on the horizon.

Sure enough, the next test reference our 91 Ford came. Somehow miraculously we were spared the loss of our car in the earlier proving time. But now I could see the storm clouds gathering on the horizon, reference this vehicle. I could not imagine being without a car. Unlike our home town in Indiana, this whole area is spread out over a vast amount of miles. No possible way, one could get by without a vehicle. As it was, we lived on the top of a mountain approximate 2.5 miles from anything. As I indicated earlier we had been blessed with an ample supply of furnishing for our house, and I could have easily sold some of the items off, to raise funds for our delinquent car payment, but there again where do you draw, the line.

God had said: "Do not sell anything to raise funds, trust me." For me to have disobeyed in this manner, I believe, it would have made the Covenant relationship null and void.

The car was more important in some ways then the apt. If need be it could become a potential shelter.

Matter of fact, I vowed at least to myself, that I would not lose this car, that I would go to work first, or least sell something to pay a payment, but when time came for me to make good on that vow. I could not bring myself to break that relationship, that had become so precious to the wife and I. Somehow, I suppose, as result of Gods' perfect timing, I was able to negotiate with the pawn shop for an additional 45 days past all deadlines, a miracle all of its own. But that too, came to a grinding halt, and they picked the car up on a Sunday afternoon, of all times, when our minister counselor friend and his wife were visiting. Even they by now were beginning to think we were wrong.

Well by now, we had no phone, no Television, other than stations we could receive without cable, however, even though we were without cable, a few times, something would be on ATB, that God would want us to see, for confirmation, and somehow we would receive a bleed over signal of ATB allowing us to watch a certain segment. It was, as if an angel was lifting the signal up to us, in order for us to receive that given message.

We could have redeemed anyone of the, afore mentioned losses in the initial beginning by selling some misc. but was unable to do so.

In the midst of all of these frustrations, and confusions shortly there afterwards, on Saturday afternoon while setting at home pondering just what we would do, The Lord whispered to me, saying: "That He was temporarily suspending The New Hope, "the church in thy house" "to allow me to become involved in fulltime evangelism, throughout the nation, and around the world. And when resuming the New Hope church it would be with a full compliment, of duties and delegated authority."

In turn, I asked: "How that could be, when I didn't even have a car?

He said: "you will see." At the conclusion, of about three weeks, an employee of the housing authority stopped by, and said: "That The Lord told her to give us her car." Well what would we do?

See Section on car

HE GIVETH MORE GRACE

1. He giveth more grace when burdens grow greater, He sendeth more strength when the labors increase to added affliction, He addeth His mercy, to multiplied trials, His multiplied peace.

2. When we have exhausted our store of endurance, When our strength has failed ere day is half done, When we reach the end of our hoarded resources, Our Father's fulfilling has only begun.

3. His love has no limit, His grace has no measure, His power has no boundary known unto men, For out of His infinite riches in Jesus he giveth, and giveth, and giveth, again.

Talk about being incommunicado, we were without any form of communications. The wife and I continued our Sunday, and Wednesday meetings, extracting with Gods' help, truths that we never knew existed. On occasion our minister friend or a neighbor would come to services, but that was few, and far between.

Somehow, I believe, by Divine origin, I happen to re-read the book The Storey's own story. So many of the things they faced, while in a concentration camp during World War II in the Philippines fit us. We literally was a prisoner of our own circumstance, and yet free to walk away at any time, but that magnetic pull from the Savior was by far more important than all this world to the both of us.

We without doubt were in that box prophesied to us earlier, for which we took a lot of heat. Many said God wouldn't do that. Albeit they didn't know the circumstances, only we did. Even the gas on the car we had, seemed to be controlled. We ran on empty more than anything.

Fortunately, I was able to get Sam Hughes, the Cadillac of all preachers, Jim Anderson, and James Delbar on the television without cable, which turned out to be our routine Sunday morning programs. The encouragement from these programs, proved to be very helpful in the test and trials that we were going through at the time.

Till now we always managed to eat good for we had a large variety of food stored up, but it too began too dwindled. With little or no cash, to buy food we begin to run low. Likewise our toiletry pantry ran dry. We come to know the meaning of Philippians 3:19 Whose God [is their] belly.

For near six, to seven months, for the most part of the time, we didn't have enough food in the house to make a meal, and yet beyond some ordained fasting, we didn't miss a meal. No, we didn't have steak, and gravy, but we had our daily portion of Manna as it were, supplied by whom ever, The Lord would send to help us, mainly neighbors.

Again Matthew 4:4 Come into focus more and more. Strangely enough God had shared with me that our obesity would be healed, and it was.

Somehow, someway, God always sent someone with food for the wife and I. Our former pastor at New Beginning had made a statement from the pulpit, saying: "That God would feed you, if He had to send the ravens to do it." Now I believe it. For, He took care of us during this time.

On one given occasion, Connie Moore was talking how caffeine, had had a bad impact upon her life, and she stated, "That she had quit drinking regular coffee."

Immediately, Satan came to me, saying: "That I was going to sin, if I drank any more coffee, consequently losing my ministry. He came against me, with all of the blackness of hell, causing me much stress to say the least, but strangely enough after praying through on the matter, God provided me, an abundance of coffee throughout the whole ordeal. That was probably one of the few things that we didn't have a shortage of.

Earlier in the year, when things begin to fall apart, the wife out of her generosity, for which I will always appreciate, offered to go to work. She has always stood by me one hundred and ten percent. But her job was to be my help mate, not my all and all supporter. My commitment to her, at marriage, was to take care of her, not her to support, or take care of me.

I stated: "That if my anointing for this faith walk, would not cover her, then it was not worth while having." As I saw it, my covenant with her at time of marriage was to support her, and I felt, that in as much, as God had told me not to hold secular employment, then it was not her job to support me, but God's job, to support the both of us. And just as I suspected, He did.

There were many invitations for the both of us to go to work, mostly for the greed and avarice of the ones who offered, hoping that we would succumb to their so called gracious offers for their own benefit, not ours.

Well I was shut up, and could not come forth. By now I seemed to be in the same predicaments my friends were when in the Philippines, before being captured by the Japanese. They had to stay hid in the day and travel at night to keep from being captured. Bro. Storey said that most of that time, he was unable to do any ministry, but spent his time memorizing scripture. Well Praise God, I now know, many verses, verbatim do to the months of imprisonment at our home.

Another interesting thing happened as I seemingly would have to while as it were my time away. God had told me in revelation: "That I had a very vivid imagination." What seemed interesting to me was in response to James Delbar comments that we must have a plan, my imagination ran wild, reference the ministry. Matter of fact it was the combination of visions, and imaginable plans, and knee-ology that has help keep this ministry alive. In revelation to me, God revealed: "That He liked vivid imaginations, and if I thought not, look at all of the little crispy creatures, that He, and His father, had created." Then He proceeded to parade, all sorts of various little creature (some I never seen before) right before my very eye.

How Great Thou Art

1. Oh Lord My God! When I am in awesome wonder consider all the World's Thy Hand have made, I see the stars, I hear the rolling Thunder, Thy power through-out the Universe display.
2. When through the woods and forest glades I wonder and here the birds sing sweetly in the trees; When I look down from lofty mountains grandeur And hear the brook and feel the gently breeze.
3. When Christ shall come with shout of acclamation and take me home, what joy shall fill my heart! Then I shall bow in humble adoration, And there proclaim, My God How Great Thou Art.

Chorus Then sings my soul, My Savior God, to Thee: How Great Thou Art, How Great Thou Art! Then sings my soul, My Savor God To Thee; How Great Thou Art, How Great Thou Art!

Well at about this time, I can hardly type for tears swelling up.
Certainly brings to my remembrance the assignment that I received while in ministry school. (Name, fifty things about a in-adament object, i.e. a flower, a bug, or any other thing that might be of interest). I believe, with all of my heart, that God wants us to just relax, and enjoy the fullness of His Glory so beautifully portrayed in every manifestation possible.
At the time of my brief visit, to what I perceived as a room just outside of the Heaven, alluded to earlier I did not sense any distractions, sadness, worry, fear, anxiety, pain, or suffering but pure glory, power, strength, goodness, and happiness, in what I can describe as the most beautiful laughter that I have ever heard.

Well I am not sure why the long tedious wait, but I have a suspicion that God wants us to trust Him only, and not worry about anything. That has been a hard lesson for me, for as I have allude too earlier, in the business world you couldn't wait for it to happen, you had to make it happened, but ministry is God's domain, and He, and He, alone is in control. 1 John 4:18

Well by now, the brook was beginning to run dry at our apt.

As I stated earlier, we had been granted a waiver of rent, but utilities and late charges had to be paid. At the time of being granted that waiver, we owed the $109.00, and had no way to pay it, except through liquidation. By this time, we had exhausted the appeals process, and we was beginning to get into late fall. I reasoned that if my rent had been waived, then at least the accrued late charges should be waived, and again appealed the ruling. The final decision came down giving us a deadline to pay it, with the explanation that we could go to any one of several helps centers and they would gladly foot the 109.00. But there again, that put us crossways with the commandment that we had received, not only at ordination but through, God Himself "Do not confess need."

A complete house full of furniture short 109.00 but unable to sell furniture to raise funds, nor seek help from any other help agency.

Do to covenant relationship

Motive and reasoning behind this thought is Luke 17:33 Mark 8:35

Would God supply this very specific need, or had the brook ran dry? Well can you imagine paying $50.00 per month rent and little or no utilities, and now a waiver for the last ten months not to pay anything That's hard to beat, anywhere in the good ole USA. Let me tell you, we did a lot of soul searching on this matter trying to get the mind of God. The only thing that we could come up with is that inner small voice, "Trust me I know what I am doing" over and over, we would seek with intensity. Alluded; too earlier, we would not have had to sell one thing, reference God's command, but still yet we would have to confess need. Many helps agencies in the area would no doubt have been glad to pay the $109.00 but for us it seemed a no. Many times in the remaining span of time, I teetered, on the brink, of using a helps agency, after all God had put me in a Government Housing project, but when it came time to do it, we couldn't break the third commandment of this covenant.

Just as I begin to blink, and yield to the temptation of confessing need the Lord brought to my memory the (vs. if you seek to save your life you will lose it) Mark 8:35

Again, the visions was running rampant reference our house on the babbling brook, and our RV, not to mention many others, yet Satan was doing his best to destroy our hope reference anything that we felt God had promised us.

He began to bombard my thoughts with doubt asking? Now why would anyone want to give you a new Lincoln town car, or new RV, or a house (in which The Lord ask me himself) on a babbling brook?

We both were, believing for all three, miracles, for months on end, and having multiple visions of the same. Over and over Satan would attempt to destroy our hope and the promises of these items. I had come into contact with many well meaning individual, who always doubted such miracles, including our x-minister friend from whom God had liberated us from. Now Satan was doing his best to destroy that hope.

Shortly after Satan's relentless bombardment, we attended a gospel sing, at a small mission in Pearl City, TN. A well know ATB. Personality Rhonda Roark was the host singer. Strangely enough, an electrical storm caused a power outage less than an hour into the sing. The sound equipment, and electrical musical instruments, became useless. Hoping for the power to come back on, the pastor called for some testimonies. At the beginning, some gentlemen, who I had never seen before, came to the front standing not more than three feet from me, looking at no one in particular, and yet looking directly at me, told of three miracles, he had just recently received. By his words, Its seems, that he happened to be meandering about his yard on that special day, and a individual, who he did not know, came up and told him he had a house to give him, overlooking Watts Bar Dam. He literally signed the deed over to him on that given day. Houses in that area start at $100,000.00 and go upward. After receiving the house, many told him they had been trying to buy the house, but the gentlemen who owned it would not sell it to them. Three days later, an individual called him on the phone, and told him to come to the Lincoln dealership, to get a new Lincoln. Thinking it was a ploy, he told the gentleman on the phone: "I have no money to buy a car, much less a Lincoln.

The gentleman told him it had already been paid for, all he had to do, was pick it up. When he showed up he received a $48,000.00 Lincoln fully paid for, including all taxes. And then he said: "That less than a week later this same gentleman showed up at his house with a pickup truck fully loaded with new bikes and toys for his grandchildren." Obviously from his testimony, he was in the same plight we were in. Wow!!! God reminded me: "That if I could do it for him, (referring to this man) I can do it for you."

What I thought was so strange, he could have received a Chevrolet, Ford, Buick, or any one of a number of other vehicles, but it was a Lincoln Town Car for which I have been believing All God ask us to do, is believe.

For the next couple months, while still in Pearl City, we started to attend this church. They only had one service on Sunday starting at 2:00 pm. enabling us to continue our night services in our home.

On another occasion when attending Revival services at this same church within the same time span, our gas tank was on empty. I had one dollar for which I was going to use for gas. Gas station is right next door to church, and I might add downhill all the way. On the way to church God whispered to my spirit saying: (see. vs. Ex. 34:20 not to appear before empty)

I said: "Lord my tank is on empty, what am I going to do? "Trust Me" He said. In obedience to the Lord's command, we put our last dollar in the offering. Now, how would we make it home? Well we made it home and back again to the gas station without running out. The Lord later revealed to me, that our willingness to comply with His request brought about a complete new equation, with new protocol, and dialogue. Asking what this meant, He stated that it had shortened the entire process by a month.

Power Building Time

Within the same period of time, while attending this church, The Lord had been referring to this walk, and comparing it to the turbulence one sees on an aircraft carrier with jets aboard, ready to be launched forward by a catapult having been held back until that right moment for it to be released and then launched into the air.

As He stated this was power building time, and that we as it were, was being held back for the purpose of power building.

I felt, that I had been maintaining this power building stance for some time, and was about ready to be launched and strangely enough while attending services at the small church, The Lord told me that I was in the air. Well I didn't know what that meant, but soon found out.

Court

That was on Sunday Oct. 13, 2002 and on Thur. 10-17-2002 I received an eviction notice from management reference our apt. The relationship: that we had maintained, between us and management was cordial. I had been in this position in my business career, as I alluded to earlier, and I well understood that they had a job to do.

Unfortunately, I couldn't comply with their request. It seemed the brook had run dry. Management was very sympathetic to our needs, and almost begged me, to go get help, but I couldn't do it. I felt that if God wanted me to stay there, then he would provide the money for me to do so. Not only did I feel that way, but I felt that He had given me ample proof of the same.

We didn't know where all of this would lead, but we felt we had no other choice but to obey.

Even after the eviction had been served, and filed, the management granted us the privilege of paying the back $109.00 and they would have dismissed the eviction suit. At the time of appearing before the Judge management stated that we could stay with the same restrictions, but now court cost and attorney fees. Well we felt sure something would come about, but God, obviously had other plans. And the wife and I wasn't' interested in circumventing them plans. Now: the same from this apartment. We didn't understand. Only God knew. In the back of our mind we well remembered what happened, the last time reference, the $2500.00.

On Oct. 31 we appeared before the judge, and he gave us 10 working days to vacate, with the understanding that we could stay, if arrearage was paid along with attorney fees. That meant we had to be out by November 14.

Like a slow motion television before our very eyes

Strangely about two weeks prior to our forced move from Maple lane, all of a sudden, I begin to see a strong vision, of as it were, a prison yard, with the two story guard tower, with lights on, and the massive razor wire topped chain link fence, with the gates closed, and Jesus standing on the inside, with the keys dangling from His hand. As time progressed to our moving date the RV, with trailer, and the Town car showed up, on the exterior, but as time came closer for moving the gates opened, and the vehicles came inside, the prison yard, and turned around facing the exterior of the prison yard. It appeared that the angels were loading the undercarriage of the RV. A day or so before our move, I woke up one morning and both vehicles were gone. Startled I begin to ask God where they were and then, He allowed me to see, that they had both been moved to the outside of the fenced in prison yard.

As stated before, this walk was much different than the other walk, requiring more faith, and trust in the master. Well Nov. 14, Thursday. Came, and we still was just as penniless, as ever, with little gas, and now faced with the possibility of being homeless. We had a complete three rooms full of relative good furniture, but still did not feel that we were released to sell it. What would we do with it? That was my one escape mechanism for raising cash. But now, that seemed out of the question. Through much prayer, we felt the Lord leading us to give it away. I said: "Lord how can that be? What will we do for money." But in obedience to the master, we gave it to the neighbor, albeit I retained the television and microwave, thinking that if all went bad we could at least sell these two items for a little pocket change. But that too became a "no" "no" for when I started to load them in the car, the Lord said: "leave them," so in obedience to Him, we left them. The only thing that we could take with us was just a few personal belongings. Being late in the evening we called management, and ask if we could at least stay till Friday and they consented. We agreed to turn the key in on Friday a day later then ordered by the court but management went along with it. Well that Friday came with still no place in mind for us to go.

That evening following our vacation, I was lead to see the police dept., who, had access to temporary housing, and they put us up in a beautiful Motel 8 for Friday and Saturday night, with money for food and the beautiful continental breakfast that they are so famous for. We ate to our hearts content, for we hadn't had access to that type food for, sometime.

This concerned me to say the least, because I felt, that we were confessing need, but when asking the Lord how that equated with my order not to confess need, "He stated that it was after the fact. He went on to say, that I had in fact played this thing out for all it was worth and now it would be His turn to provide.

Having learned our state of being, early Sunday morning, our daughter came to see us at the motel. She was very much disturbed, and broken up in as much as we were homeless again, as she stated: "For the second time." She didn't understand. She seemed to be taking it rather hard, which surprised us, as we felt that they had been greatly influenced by many individuals at the church, where we had been assistant pastor.

They had already showed their true colors. Never the less, she and her husband opened up their house to us for the second time. We did not feel that to be an option, for it is mass confusion in their place of residence. Their house is a small three bed room dwelling, with little or no room for nothing, not to mention the fact, that they have four active children, but it seemed that all other doors were closed.

In addition, our son-in-laws family lives on the same lot not more than 100ft from their house.

To add injury to insult, the son-in-laws family does not have any spiritual insights, and are quick to hurl remarks, such as: "Well we have to work for a living," or "You have to have a job to have nice things," or anyone of a hundred other remarks, for Satan to use as a weapon against us.

In addition, the grandbabies had been so dramatically influenced by the son in laws family, as well as their own parents, not to mention the many wagging tongues at the church that they themselves, even though they were only 5yrs and 6yrs old begin to make comments to us, such as: "They knew why we had to move." "They knew why we had lost the car" etc. and it went on and on.

If only they knew, the truth, but how do you tell children at that age, who have been brainwashed into thinking that their grandparents whom they love are nothing more than deadbeats. The wife and I had to give it to the Lord. Yet now we were being moved into this type of resentful atmosphere.

I suppose they got it honestly, for I had always preached, The Biblical aspect, if a man doesn't work, he shouldn't eat. Well that didn't apply to me, for I was working the best I could in ministry.

Satan had no doubt, pulled his largest guns out for this battle, and was not about to let me forget it.

Following her visit, it all of a sudden dawned on me, that we had no place to go for church. Approximately two months earlier we had been released from the Church in our house, but for lack of another place to go, we continued to have church there, and in addition attended the small mission on Sunday afternoon. Now, that did not seem to be an option. All of a sudden while contemplating what we might do The Lord said, very specifically to me: "Go to New Beginning. That was the last thing that the wife, and I wanted. It simply was out of the question, as I had already indicated earlier, they all treated us like dirt. Our lives to date hadn't changed any, and everything was in limbo as earlier, and we knew how uncomfortable we would be attending that church. But it seemed that The Lord didn't give me any other option. It was a direct demand. I said to the wife: "You are not going to believe what the Lord just told me to do" She; stated: "Go back to New Beginning Church. He had earlier told her the same. So we returned now, for the second time, to the church, that we had got booted out of.

Surprisingly, they were more, friendly then I had anticipated, but they were as yet, unawares of our latest move.

When arriving at the church, even our own family, ignored us, and set on the opposite side of the church, as if we had the plague, hardly giving us the time of day. The only one that paid us any attention was the youngest grandbaby, and he was too young to know what this thing was all about.

We were still welcomed only as seat warmers.

Following church, with no options left, we made our way to our daughter's house. She had stated earlier, that they had prepared one of the bedrooms for us. That was far from what we wanted, but at least it was a place to stay.

The only thing we seemed to have an abundance of, for the time being, was gas. Thank goodness for that, for their house was approximately fifteen miles from the New Beginning church. For the first week we were there, gas was in abundance, but too it seemed to dwindle. The wife, and I, enjoyed the few short trips we could make on the limited gas we had, mostly to church. For months, we hadn't been out of the city limits, of Pearl City. When one has been in this predicament for the length of time we had been, you tend to be very careful, not to waste resources such as gas. Maybe not a faith producing thought.

Following our move, our diets, improved considerable, for as I had alluded to earlier, we were as it was living on manna, which effectively sustained us, just as it did the children of Israel, but far from the leeks, and garlic, they were so accustomed too, in Egypt.

The devil, many times, while on this manna diet, paraded before our very eyes, many of the delicacies such as pizza, long Johns Silvers fish, hamburgers, Pepsis, and every other thing, that we had been so used to eating. He continually tried his best to stop us in this walk, but failed miserably, thanks to the grace of God. From time to time we would go the grocery store, and walk up and down the aisle I suppose just to look at the delicious food for which we didn't have any money, to buy. It reminded me of James Moran's trip to the Crispy Cream donut factory, while on a 40 day fast. He just wanted to see how strong his will power would be without yielding to his special love for pastries. Well he overcame, and so did we.

We both, had lost a considerable amount of weight, and I was able to wear my old wedding suit. To God, Be the Glory! The Lord, had told me many times, in revelation, that He was going to give me the strength of my youth, even as it was in a photo taken at 212 N Main, when I was in the prime of my life, at age 28. Well now, I was down to the same size thanks to God.

By now Thanksgiving was upon us, and still we were penniless. We had always been used to having large dinners, but now for the second year, it seemed as though we would have no large dinner. But as always, The Lord takes care of His, own. Strangely enough, even though our son in laws mother, vowed not to have a dinner, her five children: raised up in opposition to her, and coerced her into having a good meal, at our daughters house. Being there, we were a part of that. It seemed as though The Lord was fattening us up, at the expense of somebody else, certainly not us.

In as much, as our son in laws mother doesn't like to cook, the wife was in charge of making noodles, and much of the balance of the menu, consequently, the dinner we had, came close to being the same as when having our own dinner.

Not only was she in charge of just this dinner but she was in charge of doing all the cooking within the house, as the daughter does not like to cook.

Well that Thanksgiving Day came and went, with a lot of frustration, in as much, as we were seemingly stuck in a place, full of resentment, having to listen to the varied remarks, as to the reasons we were there. But Gods grace was sufficient...

Well time continued to drag on, and I thought much about what Connie Moore had said: "Enjoy the walk through the valley."

Well, no doubt, we were still in the valley,

By now, our minister, and councilor friend, had found out that we had moved to the daughter's house, and paid us a visit. He again likened our move to being in the house of "Obed Edom."

As stated earlier they had no doubt been pulled away from us, for Whatever reason, perhaps forcing us to walk this walk alone.

By now they begin to feel that perhaps we were on the wrong track.

Concerned he told us: "That perhaps it might be in your best interest to go to work, if need be," but he simply did not understand.

Out of desperation to help us, his wife wanted to know why we didn't share our need with them, for the $109.00 to keep us in the apt., again no explanation would satisfy them so we didn't try.

One thing that I will always be confident about is that they continually kept us in their prayers, and unlike so many others, did not go behind our back as others had. Still yet today, we continue to fellowship with them.

Well it seemed to be as if we were in a half way house with limited freedom. At least by being there, we had access to cable television allowing us to watch our beloved ATB, and my news program, plus I had access to my son in laws computer.

Our gas supply, had dwindled down to nothing, and the daughter had just purchased a newer van which would only accommodated the six of them, and maybe one other individual. The law: partially responsible for that. They were very particular, about making sure, that their van wasn't overloaded with passengers, especially with us. For some reason, they remained at arm's length with us throughout our whole stay.

As earlier stated they attended the same church we did, The New Beginning, at least 15 miles away but yet, refused to let us ride with them forcing us to drive our own vehicle.

That was all well and fine, but it was the cold, distant, and resentful attitude and atmosphere, that we both were living in that seem to worsen as the days went by. On many occasions the son in laws family would crowd into the daughters van, and that was all well and fine, but for us they made it well known that they didn't have room to hall us, using the law as the reason.

By now we were in the Christmas season. Would this thing abate during the season, as it had the other years except last year, or would it continue on through this Christmas season as well? Well time would tell. The first test came when all four grandbabies were involved in the church Christmas program, and a Christmas dinner afterwards. They were excited about the Christmas season, and the upcoming program. The frenzy about the house was all Christmas. For the few weeks we were there, we would always leave for church, long before the rest of the family, but now this Sunday, we lingered, because we did not have enough gas to get to church, certainly timed just like the devil wanted. So off they went to the Christmas services with not only them, but part of the son in laws family with them, in their van, that wasn't large enough to haul us, and there we set. Some would argue that God wasn't supplying our needs, but that is rather debatable. Well, it was certainly frustrating to say the least, especially to the wife, as she tends to get wrapped up in this sort of thing. So we did, as we had been so used to doing, we had church in the house and continued our faith walk as best we could.

When the family came home, the first crack out of the 11 year old grand-daughters mouth was: "Thanks for the support." No doubt brought on by the parents.

They all wanted to know why, we didn't come to church. We told them, that we had no gas. The daughter, ask us why we did not tell them, and I said: "We did not feel to express need." Well for the balance of the time, we were at their, house they would always give us gas money for going to church.

By now Christmas had arrived, and we were still penniless, as before.

The son in law, and daughter, did see fit to take us out to Pizza Hut, for a meal, but that too seemed to be marred with resentment.

Well again, we had another large Christmas, dinner, that was brought in by various family members, with the exception of the small basket the daughter received from the church.

We still were unable to buy any presents for each other, the children, or grandbabies. The wife didn't feel it necessary to explain to the grandbabies, as before, feeling that it would only worsen the matter. So there we set, with Christmas exchanges going around about us, and we couldn't even get off of the premises.

Still yet, our resolve became stronger than ever, as we did not fail, or break The Covenant.

Well visions continued to be more prevalent, and stronger than ever, but nothing reference them happened. Habakkuk 2:3

By now we was coming into the New Year season, with things as dead as ever. As alluded to earlier the wife, and I, had begin to feel the coldness, tension, and resentment, at us being there, for there were times, that it was all we could do to stay, but where would we go with no money. Fortunately, or unfortunately, for us at the beginning of each day, at first light, most of the family would head over to the in laws family residence, leaving us by our selves One would have thought we had the plague. But again we had the run of the house, while they were gone.

One day in particular, the daughter came home screaming: "I don't know what is going on, but you better find some type of a job, for I just got a $400.00 light bill," as if we had something to do with it.

I said: "We can leave if you want us to." She said: "I didn't say that," I went on to say: "I can probably get you some help with the bill," She said: "I don't want help, I just want money." Then she stormed out. Very much in evidence that she was being coerced, by whom ever.

Well mid-January came and all of a sudden, one night, the same vision came back to me reference the prison gates. I mentioned this to the wife, wondering if that meant we might have to move again, but only speculation. By now, most of the family was staying at the In-laws residence, all but for sleeping, which was well with us.

Within the next few days, the daughter, sent the oldest granddaughter, age fifteen, to give us a note. She was, requesting, that we find another place. She said: "The pressure was just too great." She stated: "That she did not alone, own the house, and that she had agonized over the decision, and that it was final." She put no timetable on it. She did not want us to talk with her about it, threatening to end it immediately, if we dare ask any questions about it. Corresponding through the grandbabies, the only way, she reluctantly gave us a week to get out. Well she was none the happier then we were it appeared the brook had run dry.

David Crabtree repeatedly stated there is a process that one must follow in this type thing, so we had to play it to the end, or as it were till the brook ran dry. Yes at anytime, we could have walked away from it, but then what. The final week dragged on with little or no change, to the general living conditions. The son in law, had started smoking again, and always when we would leave the house, he would start smoking in the house, and we felt that if for some reason, we didn't heed there notice to move, he no doubt, would have used that as a way to get us to leave. There is nothing worse, than a house full of cigarette smoke to a non smoker.

Vision of Betty Burnette, Strangely enough before this all happened, I begin to see Ms. Burnette's in a vision for several days. I mentioned to the wife, but didn't know the reason. Shortly thereafter, I happened to be surfing the channels, and I just happened to turn to ATB, not my regular time to watch ATB and there she was. The first words out of her mouth that day was don't, jump out of the boat, You will be glad you didn't. I certainly had entertained the idea many times, that if this thing didn't abate shortly, that I would not quit serving the Lord, but perhaps, I was on the wrong track, not to mention the fact that Satan had reminded me many times, as almost every other individual, I knew, that I was on the wrong track.

Well as always the Lord has a way to bolster your faith when all seems bad.

In the same program, she began to tell of various faith incidents, of Gods faithful provisions. I remembered of some of her earlier remarks

In which God had told her to speak to a cash machine even though there was no money in her account, and she received the amount she had spoken to the machine.

She told of incidents relating to her gas tank, when near empty, such as finding money near the pumps etc. Well at the time, I thought that all sounded strange but there again I had seen some strange things in the last four years.

See Luke 5:26

Faith walk with the gas tank—One morning shortly before our move from the daughters, The Lord woke me up, and told me, that He wanted me to go to Knoxville, which is a distance of about 65 miles, one way. I said: "Lord my gas tank is on empty, and I have no money to buy gas with."

He said: "I know that, but I want you to speak to the gas tank."

Startled I said: "What might I say to the gas tank,"

He said: "Gas tank be full," Well that didn't seem to me, to be a very viable solution, but there again, with the magnetic attraction of The Lord, one does not have the will power to say no. It was cold, and I had no money in my pocket, and I knew that if I ran out of gas the only possible way, I could get some gas was to sell something for which I had very little left.

As I told Him: "I didn't feel like chasing around in the cold for gas." But still yet, I felt that tug, and that inner voice saying: "Trust me I know what I am doing." After a struggle in the battle field of the mind, I and the wife left for Knoxville. There was a gas station 3.8 miles from the house, and I knew I had enough to get there.

I, in fact stopped at the station, hoping I would find some money near the pumps as Ms. Burnette had talked about, but none was available. I even went into the station, thinking that perhaps someone might have been told to give me some gas money, but that all proved to be nothing. Needless to say, I was shaking in my boots, and wanted to return home, but probably didn't have enough gas to even do that. So I and the wife elected to continue on toward Knoxville, on an empty tank.

As we pulled away from the station, I said: "Lord now it is yours, I have done what you told me." I guess, at any moment, I expected to run out of gas, for the gas gage said empty, but it just kept going. On in to Knoxville we went. We headed for the Lincoln dealership, spending more time then what we had anticipated, and even obtained a quote. All the while, I was as nervous, as an old sitting hen. Following that, He wanted me to go to another Lincoln dealer on the other side of town, for an additional quote, but by that time, I was in no mood, to look further, as I was only concerned about how, and if I would make it home. Having looked at the Lincolns we made our trek home, again expecting to run out of gas. But we continued on, until we got approximate ten miles from home, and I begin to feel the car gasping for gas. The wife and I, begin to pray reminding The Lord of what He had told me, and we continued to keep going, all the while, the car continued to gasp for gas. We continued on past the gas station, that we had earlier stopped at, and approximate two miles from home, our engine died, right in front of a drive way allowing me to pull into the drive way, from the busy road.

I said: "Lord what do we do now"

He replied: "Trust me, I know what I am doing" As I looked up, there was a lady working out in the yard, (mid-winter), and I approached her, telling her, that I was out of gas, and asked, if I might leave my car there until I could get some.

She says: "I have gas in the garage, I will get you some." When checking it, she found out that it had been mixed with oil for a lawn mower, and so she immediately stated, that she would go to the station approximately 1.5 miles away to get some.

I said: "I don't have any money on me, for which to pay you,

She said: "That is ok, I will get, you a couple of gallons. Just count it a blessing from The Lord." Having gone to the station, she purchased two gallons of gas, enough to get me home, and back to the station. Well again God had miraculously supplied our gas and got us to the exact place, and re-supplied us with more.

I asked: "The Lord why he allowed me to run out of gas." He responded; "I wanted you to know how much you had left for your next trip."

This type thing occurred three different times, while living in this area, and each time the Lord supplied the means for me to get gas, not costing me a dime.

Well by now the brook had run dry, and it was time to heed the daughter request. As stated earlier, we felt that they would use cigarette smoke as a method to get us out of the house, if we prolonged our stay, not to mention the fact of the coldness and distance that the wife and I felt.

The wife had always helped get the children off to school each morning and the Friday, January 31, 03 was no different. Two days before, the daughter in our presence, had told the two boys, the 5 yr old, and 7 yr old, that we were leaving, but refrained from any other comments. On Friday, the two boys did not want to go to school, and the 15yr old, granddaughter who the daughter had used to give us the moving note remained home. But all were ordered to stay in bed. The daughter knew that we would be leaving early that morning and she apparently did not want them up. The wife and I, finished loading our car, and just as soon as Connie Moore went off, on ATB we headed out for the wild blue yonder, strangely enough with a little peace, and yet frustrated that the daughter did not have the decency to get up and tell us by. As it turned out the two boys 5&6 were the only ones that willingly told us bye, as even the 15yr old had to be coerced into doing so. Not a very good send off.

We had just watched a program Little House on the Prairie in which Doc. Baker had to leave under adverse conditions, and not one of his friends showed up to bid him bye

No sooner than we had left, The Lord reminded me of just how fragile family ties can be, and reminded me, of how regretful almost to the point I was, of breaking our Covenant Relationship with The Lord in order that we might buy the family Christmas. He reminded me, that there is nothing, not even family, that is worth breaking a relationship with Christ for. How grateful the wife and I were, that we did not yield to temptation. I believe that this was just another test to prove our faithfulness to The Lord Jesus.

01-31-03

Well with no place else to go, I felt lead to go to the Disciple Center (after the fact) for at least counsel. I made contact with Bob Trees who I thought was the manager, but found out he was no longer the manager. However he did introduced me to the manager, and likewise made the new manager aware of my efforts to work within the program when I was yet assistant pastor, and also made him aware of the fact that I had taken in a man direct from jail, in an effort to help him.

This greatly enhance my favor with the new manager, and he assisted us by giving us an additional three nights lodging again in Super 8 Motel, along with food, and gas. As it was, the motel was just down the road from New Beginning, and so we attended their on Sunday, with little or no response from our family, beyond the 5yr old. In fact, none of the family would even come near us. While we can't be sure, much whispering was being made, I am sure about us, and the unusual circumstances that we were in again homeless, with no place to go. We felt sure that they had been coerced into doing what they did by some of the church members, as well as other members of the son in laws family. There again Satan plays a big role in causing our mind to run rampant in this type thing. Needless to say, we did not enjoy the services that day, and brought to remembrance, the statement I had heard so often, how can you minister to someone who is in this type of position without first ministering to their needs. Well for the next three glorious days we had beautiful facilities at the Super 8 motel with their continental breakfasts. We received a lull in the storm for this time.

By now I was beginning to be well acquainted 1 John 4:18 no fear in Love.

For the past few months, we had heard advertisement on television of the homeless shelters being full, having to turn people away. We had never given much thought of having to spend any time in a shelter such as this, believing that we might be spared such a misfortune.

At the time of our departure from Maple Lane, the manager, in an effort to help us, had recommended that we go to the Kingston Rescue Mission but that was not on our list of favorite things to do. She even stated how sad she was, that something did not work out for us. She believed the Lord would work something out, but obviously that was not in His pre-determined will. So with her hands tied she bid us farewell.

On Monday morning following our stay in the Motel 8 facilities, I again contacted Bob Trees for council. From his experience with the

The Disciple Center he knew that they would be unable to help us any, more, and he suggested that we go to the rescue mission indicating that they had new facilities. Of course every one that we came into contact with had always suggested that we go get a job. I have no trouble believing, that in fact, if I had been cleared to get a job, I probably could have got three jobs a day, but that is not what God had told me. As alluded to earlier, we had given up all, of our license, in response to The Lords request, and we was not about to cave in at no cost. Now it seemed another critical testing was looming on the horizon. With little or no choice, the wife and I, headed to the last place we ever wanted to go, The Kingston Rescue Mission. We had all kinds of thought what that might entail but tried to cast it out of our mind. The wife was highly upset, and agitated, thinking perhaps that we would not be able to stay together. Not to mention of the ghostly stories that we had heard about, and seen on TV. But God loves them also. In fact while assistant pastor, I had visited the mission and it was certainly far from what I wanted. But as I have come to discover, since being in the ministry it's "YES LORD," not my will but "THINE." Only God now seemed to be in control.

Well we made the 65 mile trek to the mission on that fateful first day of February, not knowing what to expect. Probably one of things that had prepared my mind for this is the three mission trips that I had taken. Many of the mission stations are far from what we Americans are used too. In most instances they do not have the luxury of American life style that we all enjoy so tremendously. But as I stated before God is no respecter of persons and has extended HIS call to the world.

KINGSTON RESCUE MISSION 01-31-03

We arrived just after dinner, and after having been interviewed, and accepted by the case manager, we come to learn, that our timing of being there was critical, for we got the last room available in the family section. We both were surprised, when we viewed the room. It was just like we had left at the motel. A nice private bath, with a well furnished room, and plenty of privacy. We moved our few, meager possession in, and proceeded to get acclimated to our new surroundings. Not bad so far. Established meal times were 6:45 am., 11:45 a.m., and 4:45p.m. For the balance of that Friday, Saturday, and Sunday, we spent the time just getting acclimated to the new, but strange environment. The staff, and inmate population, graciously accepted us. One of the requirements for living there was the mandate of doing chores, and to attend the various addiction, and/or dependency meetings, and general functional meetings. The staff was responsible for the supervision of the inmates, or clients as they are called, and they do the actual work. That can range from cleaning, cooking, laundry, yard maintenance etc. Well the week following, they assigned the wife various chores, but refrained from assigning me any chores until scheduling me an appointment with the doctor, because of back problems. Beyond the general chores etc. the most repressive rule of all, was to abide by the time limits reference leaving the facility. Phase 2, program, for which we were in allowed us to be gone no more than 30 minutes per day. As you go to the higher level of phases, you are granted more time away from the facility. Primarily this rule is established for the benefit of the addicts, who when having too much time on their hand find it suitable to return to their old habits.

Having left maple lane, and the last nine months of wilderness experience references our daily food rations etc., and then moving to our daughter house, in which the daily menu had improved considerably, or at least more in concert with what we generally ate, this place was a picnic. But now the food that the rescue mission served was beyond imagination. Every conceivable type of food, one could want, you had. Unlimited: meat, vegetables, fruit, coffee, and milk. Not to mention the fact, The Lord gave us favor with one of the other residence, and every evening, she would always take the wife and I, to the fast food deli, across the street, and buy us drinks, ice cream, and snacks of all sought. The crispy cream donut factory, provide box after box of every conceivable type of pastry one could imagine. Unbelievable

For the month we were there, I put on a whapping 20 lbs. Life was great on the family side of the facility, but now we also begin to see the plight of the homeless. The mission has a policy not, to turn any,

Individual, away in the general residence section, as we were in, it consisted primarily of men and women with addictions, and a few homeless people such as we were, with no place to go, so far as housing, It technically is dedicated for helping the plight of the addicted. The number of the non-residence (the actual street people, as they are called,) varied considerably, depending on the temperature. The last night we were there, they housed a 178 street people, from every conceivable problem's going. The non-residence was, allowed to eat all three meals each day, on the premises, but must leave the premises after meal time. In the evening, following the night meal, they are immediately escorted to a separate quarters for baths, and bedding. They are tightly scrutinized.

The week following our arrival, The Lord woke me up in the middle of the night, and reminded me of Psalms 23, Yea though I walk through the valley of the Shadow of death, and then reminded me, of the fact that not only was I walking through that valley, but likewise, I was observing the fate of others, who were doing the same thing, with not knowing our Lord. And then, He went on to say: "That the two of us, referring to Him, and His Father as One, and I and Ms. Judy as one, was going to walk up and down the corridors of the earth preaching His Gospel to every Tongue, Tribe, Kindred, and Nation under the Sun." And then, He said: "Open your eyes," and when I did, He, was as it were, holding the globe, in the palms of His hands, with Angels on either side pointing to it. That got my attention in a hurry. I couldn't believe it. And then the Key word, He seem to give me, was "Observation." Gut wrenching to say the least. The affects of sin on these individuals life, was horrible almost to the point of non-describable.

I wish, that every teen who has the temptation, be it ever so small, to use tobacco, alcohol, in any form, or drugs of any type, could see where the ends of this road leads.

While being spared the plight of knowing where to hang our hat, for beyond three to four hours at the most, it is most troubling to just wander with no where you can call home. We was on DIVINE ASSIGNMENT and knew that The Lord would take care of us, but these poor people of every age, was there because of the lure of sin in their life, and not being acquainted with THE MASTER.

Now the Lord reminded me very vividly of Isa. 43:1,2 Here the wife and I were right in the midst of this misery, and plighted conditions, but yet we had suitable, far more than expected privacy, with good housing similar to the motel, that we had left.

Well again the vision of the prison gate showed up again. Immediately following our arrival at the mission, the vision of the prison gate had disappeared. Now approximate three weeks into our stay, I woke early one morning, and there it was again. I immediately recalled the last two times that I had received that vision and that within just a short time we had to move. We had no idea, as to how long we might have to stay, but felt sure, time was on our side. As I have stated so frequently we are more or less just biding time. The Lord has told me, so frequently: "Stay close to me, Keep your eyes off of the storm, and on me." It is well documented in Holy writ reference Peter taking his eyes off of the Master for a short time and when he did, he began to sink.

Within this environment, it would have been very easy to get our mind off the Master and on the storm, but we couldn't do that. Fortunately for the both of us, when the wife's spirit was up, my spirit was down, when her spirit was down, my spirit was up. In our materialistic age, at all levels of society, all emphasis is placed on man's ability to defend for his self with little or no dependence on God. People do not believe that God is the same, yesterday, today, and forever, oh yes they say they do, but when push comes to shove, they quickly change directions, and scoff at the ones who do feel that way. As the Lord reminded me, don't cast your pearl before swine. Matthew 7:6

The wife and I, both found out, that it did little good to discuss our faith walk with any one, but a select few, for immediately they put up a strong wall of negativism against you, consequently affecting ones faith level.

And that was the case with one self described theologian, and counselor on the staff, at the mission, who admittedly had a MA degree in religion. He boasted of having written a thesis on the book of Job, but still refuted most of the information with in that book, and about what I was saying, and blatantly and openly criticized me for my belief saying: "that I was not Elijah."

As I have steadfastly stated: "Either God's Word is true or it's not."

And this place was no exception. Even though this was a Christian mission, little emphasis was placed upon dependence upon our Lord.

Many, of the so called Christian counselors scoffed at the idea of faith which requires total and complete dependence upon God.

I am not discounting the fact, that man does have a part to play, that being faith, love, and obedience, wrapped in a garment of Praise, and short of that, God is in control. I am reminded while writing this of Jesus' sayings reference John 10:18, He had the power to lay His life down, no one could take it from Him and likewise He had the power to pick up.

Albeit when one follows a faith walk, such as we were walking (bared out by stories of other faith teachers), there is, as Holy Writ, declares, obedience unto death so far as earthly rudiments and flesh is concerned. Galatians 2:20, and 2 Corinthians 6:9

At this point in time, we felt that we were at that point, of total and complete dependence, upon The Lord. There was very little we could do about our circumstance of homelessness, or the plight, for which we was in, short of doing what God had told us not to do. That: being, go to work at secular employment. As the wife, and I, discussed many times, we had given up all of our licenses for the ministry, we had invested our life's savings into this ministry, consequently The Bank of Heaven, and if by chance, we were wrong, it would take us 15 years, well past retirement age to just get back to the beggarly elements of a mundane life style. So far as we both felt, we were on a one way road to our entire D day port-folio, not about to be deterred. We did not feel, and still do not feel at time of writing, that we need to justify our faith walk and pilgrimage to no one. The key issue the Lord reminds me of, is: "If you were wrong you would not be being provided for." We would have starved to death, but that was far from the case. We would in fact, have no place to hang our hats. Again, that was far from the case. All was in limbo bills etc.

While at the mission, we were privileged to attend a Church of God in Knoxville for the duration of our stay.

Timing: based on the teachings of other faith teachers, is critical to this type of walk and if nothing more we was sure learning how to wait. Connie Moore had given a very timely example of this reference the butterfly which was prematurely cut loose from its cocoon, indicating that because of the premature birth it was never able to fly. We certainly did not want this to happen.

Three weeks end

Probably one of the worse problems I had to deal with, while at the mission, was the imprisonment, as it were, free to walk away, but yet not able to. The mission is situated within 200 ft of I-40 & I-75 downtown skyway, at Knoxville, and the constant hum of the traffic, both night and day, gave me the travel bug so bad, that I could hardly resist the temptation to get on the road and just go. It certainly brought back many memories, of the two years we was on the road In evangelism, not to mention the fact, I feel God had shown us, by this time, that we now would be on the road. And so we continued the waiting game.

Well by now the weekend had passed and on Monday we had made an appointment with the counselor about a given problem for Wednesday afternoon knowing that we had a parent training class early Wednesday morning. We always like to attend the classes for each attendee received $5.00 plus a bus ticket. So we were quick to attend the classes. On Tuesday I happened to stop by the counselor's office for council, on something, and she quickly informed me that we needed to change our appointment on Wednesday for 9:30 am. I told of the cross scheduling but she indicated that we needed to comply. She had very much urgency in her voice. Somehow I had that gut instinct within me that told me, we would be moving. The wife said that was not possible for we had done nothing wrong, but never the less, I reminded her of the repeated vision of the prison gate.

Well sure enough come Wednesday morning the counselor indicated that we would have to leave the facility by 3:00 pm. that Friday. That came as quite a shock to say the least. We attempted efforts to remain until being better equipped to leave, but it seemed the brook had run dry. They said: "They could not justify our continued residence, as we did not have any addiction problems." They did give us leave to stay at night in the non residence area, but I have already alluded to, what life would be like in this instance, not to mention the fact, that the wife and I, would have to remain alone from each other for duration of our stay at night. That was not favorable circumstances. If one ever needed each other, it was during these trying times, if for nothing more, then support. See 1 Cor. 10:13

With two day's advance notice, where would we go? I was in strange territory, not to mention, I was unfamiliar with any of the helps programs available to one, with this type problem. We had no idea to say the least, what we would do. The first thing one wants to do is to panic, but we was standing on God's Word 1 John 4:18, and Psalms 91.

In this particular instance, the wife became rather panicked but with God's strength, she was able to overcome it.

One of the reasons, I feel God allowed us to be moved from this facilities, was the fact that the one resident, who I alluded to earlier, who the Lord had given us favor with, begin to question our reasoning, reference our faith walk I.e., not consenting to government assistance, with food stamps, even a monthly allotment, along with housing. She had a brother in similar circumstances, so she knew the possibilities that lay ahead. She could see no wrong in this stance for us to do so, and became rather assertive, pressuring the wife and I, to re-think our position, in light of the pending homelessness we faced again.

Till now, she had been very helpful to the wife and I for the past three weeks, having a very powerful and assertive influence on the wife, and at times even me. When one is struggling, as we were, it could be a very attractive thought to think in such terms, but we were not there for that purpose. Nor had we come into this walk for that purpose.

As stated earlier, we had declined all efforts to get government assistance, i.e. food stamps, welfare pensions, etc. feeling that if we had to do this, then God would not be in what we were doing. After all this was a faith walk and He was providing our every basic need.

As stated earlier, we was led to accept government housing, and feel very strongly that God used this program for our assistance, but it was Him, that put us in the housing program, and not we ourselves. And He, certainly had made no effort, nor do I think He would have helped us to get food stamps, and welfare benefits, although we would have qualified for them, in light of what we were doing, when we were able body individuals very capable of doing work, but refused for reasons earlier stated.

The assertive influence, although well intentioned, begin to cause doubts and fear, in the wife, and at times even me, consequently, causing tension between us. Well, all of a sudden, I begin to feel a tremendous surge of praise coming over me, feeling at times ecstatic, that we were moving, although I had no earthly idea why, or where we might end up. The Lord had given total peace, and trust in Him.

Peace, Peace Wonderful Peace

1. Far away in depth in my spirit, to night rolls a melody, sweeter then song and celestial like strains it unceasingly falls O'er my soul like an infinite calm.
2. What a treasure I have in this wonderful peace, buried deep in my heart of my soul., so secure that no power can mine it a way, while the years of eternity roll.

Chorus Peace peace wonderful peace, coming down from the father above: Sweep over my spirit forever, I pray, In fathomless billows of love.

As I stated earlier, I had received many visions of the RV, The Lincoln Town Car, and the House on the babbling brook, not to mention the other visions that seem to be stronger than ever. By now, they were all playing as it were before my very eyes, like a television.

Perhaps, this was the time, we would get our RV. In such case it would eliminate the need for housing. I must confess, I didn't know but somehow, I knew God would take care of us.

Our friend, still suffering from the stress, and anxiety, from the quick moving notice, that we had received, continued to worry on our behalf even to the point of tears. She now was full of relentless question of just what would we do, and where we would go. Nothing I said could appease her, and likewise, the wife became even more frustrated, then normal because of our friends persistence that we must work out these problems on our own. Our friend, nor my wife, could see any interest on my part, to find housing.

As I told her: "There is very little if anything, we could do at this late date to find shelter." "It would have to be God, as we knew not what to do." Under pressure from the wife, to do something, I did check a few places but all doors were closed. We were well known within the shelter, and our friend had enlisted several other individuals, to aid us, in trying to help us find shelter throughout Thursday, but to no avail.

Our friend had continually stressed as others did, that we had to put legs to our prayers, that we just couldn't set back, and let God do it. At times, I could agree with that, but somehow, I knew that wasn't the case now, as we were facing, as it were the Red Sea. We had done all we could do, and now it was God's turn. In an effort to silence our friend, and appease my wife, I asked her: "Just how much, men played in the deliverance of, Shadrach; Meshach; and, Abednego?"

Well as you know, they had no part in their deliverance, It was God, and God only, and now He was about to deliver us.

Well! I didn't know what, but I knew something was at hand.

Thursday evening we went to bed, as usual, and slept like a log, with no worry about tomorrow. Isn't that what God tells us in

Mathew 6:33-34.

Well, we were doing all we knew to do, although shut up from ministry, but after all, God was in control. Satan was quick to remind me, that I was wrong, but God kept him far away from us that night, allowing the wife and I to sleep, with much ease.

Friday morning we awoke as usual knowing what lay ahead, but peace kept flooding my soul. At 8:00 AM, the earliest possible time, one of the ladies that our friend had enlisted to help us, with finding a place, since as our friend said: "she could see that I wasn't going to call," just happened to remember a shelter in Harriman TN. area. She immediately telephoned the office, and found that there was vacancy. She immediately put me on the phone, to make the arrangements.

Strangely enough, God always uses the least likely individuals to provide resources, and this was the case that day. For the last two days, this one particular lady kept saying that she was going to give us some money to help us out, but till now, she had made no effort to do so. We have run across many good intentioned individuals, who would say, that they was going to help us out, but that is as far, as it went. Well, we figured the same with this lady, but much to our surprise, as I was making some last minute arrangements, with not a penny in my pocket, this lady took the wife to the bank, and gave her sixty dollars. With that money, we made the 45 mile trip to Harriman. By Three PM, that same day we were in our new quarters.

Trinity Shelter Harriman 02-28-03 to 04-04-03

This shelter was owned and operated by the Holly Charities, out of Knoxville, and was located in the main part of Harriman TN. The general setting, was far more serene, then the one that we had come from.

This shelter was totally different then the mission in Knoxville. It was less repressive, but chores were still a part of the process. All cooking was done by residents, and in as much as we were the only couple there the wife cooked all of our meals. Later when the shelter became full, each resident was appointed a certain time to cook, for all of the residents. On given nights, various local churches would provide the meals. The shelter was well blessed, with an over abundance of food. One of the chores, the wife took on, while staying there, was to clean and straighten up the food pantry. No regulations were in place reference the food pantry. It was scattered over a large area, complicating any inventory control.

In one instance, I personally counted over 300 cans of green bean's alone, which were strewn over the entire storage area, and that was the same with all canned or packaged foods. Management seemed to overlook this critical problem. On behalf of the shelter population's health, all food should be dated, and used in accordance with them dates. I am a salsa lover, and on one given occasion (not at this shelter), I opened a jar of salsa, and begin to eat some of it, but noticed that it was an off color. When checking the date, I found it to be almost four years outdated.

And so it was with much of the food. In short this shelter didn't know what they had, because of the miss-management of this critical resource.

From time to time, some needy person would stop by to pick up some needful items but that too was limited by a director, and staff, who could have cared less, about anyone in these dire circumstances. They seemed to be in it for a salary only, with little or no care for any one.

The same could be said for furniture and appliances, and all household wares.

The shelter received a large quantity, of this type items, and without casting blame on anyone, we come to learn that much of it disappeared through the cracks, if you know what I mean. If the general public only knew they would be appalled.

The management was not the least bit happy to find out, that I would not hold secular employment. I told the management, of my stance reference secular employment, but like all the others, she didn't agree with me.

She told of one of her siblings, who likewise was involved with ministry, and she stated: "They worked fulltime jobs, and ministered on the side." She felt that I should do the same.

The management, had given us a month stay, and indicated that they were not in the habit of extending a stay, except we find employment. All residents were continually reminded of their remaining time, by it being posted on a chalk board in the foyer for everyone to see. Intimidating: to say the least.

As my time begin to dwindle down, and after several so called counseling sessions, on the ethics of work, the manager, took it upon herself, to schedule me an appointment with an individual, who I found out, upon my arrival, to be a head shrink, and a preacher of all things.

Well he was surprised to find out that I was a minister, and abruptly let it be known, that he used to be involved with a faith walk, similar to mine, and that it didn't pan out to be like he thought it should be, and went on to say that he had found a better way, then investing his all, in the kingdom of God. I thought of the rich young ruler, and Mark 8:36-37.

While at this shelter, we were privileged, to attend a Church of God which proved to be very helpful.

One of the things that really attracted us to this church was the powerful praise and worship services. Words could not adequately express the power of God we felt in these services. Certainly with the storms the wife and I, was going through, we needed this in our life, at this time. A few of the members, even bonded with us, even though they didn't understand the reasoning behind our walk. One caring young lady took it upon herself, after finding out that we had an upcoming anniversary gave us a $40.00 meal ticket at the Cracker Barrel.

And still yet, another couple took us out for a meal at a Mexican restaurant in the Harriman area. This same couple having learned of my previous Real Estate experience, tried to set me up with a local realty company managing a number of apartments, in exchange for a place to live, and a small salary. Having done that, and been there, I let it be known that I was not interested is such a venture, in as much as the Lord had commanded me not to be involved with secular employment. When making our divine orders known, they promptly lost interest in us, and dismissed us as a, elcrazo, or a stumble bum looking for a free ride.

But it was not the same with the pastor and his wife, Rev., and Mrs. Jim Stone, for our spirits immediately bonded, and he continued to give us a warm welcome.

Towards the end of our stay, at the shelter, he asked us to preach on a Wednesday night. Likewise in as much as he was a general overseer of several churches, in the area, he wanted me to take one, but didn't have any vacancies at the time.

Much to my surprise, he contacted another general overseer, knowing that he had an upcoming vacancy, and even sent me to Lafollette, TN. to discuss that possibility, with him, but that effort proved to be futile, as the pastor of that given church was unsure about his continuation as the pastor. I believe it was not Gods timing.

By now, our time had dwindle down to the last three days Wed. Thurs. & and on Friday we was to be out.

On Wednesday evening, we received an invite, to preach at the church the following Wednesday night, but wondered if I could do so, because, I was unsure as to where I would be at. The next day, I ask the manager of the shelter, of the possibility of me staying till the following Friday, because of the invite to preach. She screamed at me: "somehow I knew you were going to ask me for additional time, I don't know why I am doing this, but yes you can stay till the following Friday." Thinking of Dan 4:35, I laughed inwardly. She just could not understand it, and was very irate to say the least. Well! The speaking fee, provide me with gas money for our next move, for which we didn't know where.

By now, I begin to see the prison gate, but as of now it was closed, and did not start opening, till Monday of the following week.

By this time, another couple had arrived at the shelter, for which we became well acquainted. The Lord, always raised someone up, to help us in various ways, whatever that need might be. To God, Be the glory! When finding out of our near moving date she just happened to remember of having lived at a small one room shelter, owned and operated by the Wood Lock Ministerial Assn., approximately ten miles south of Harriman, TN. She likewise gave us the name of pastor, Bill Bradley, who was the head of the RMA building. When calling the Rev. Bradley he scheduled an appointment with me, for the same day, and graciously accepted us, for a, thirty day tenure, to be reviewed every ten days. And so on that following Friday, with the prison gate opened, we headed south to the small town of Wood Lock. We had another place to hang our hat for the time. And just before moving this same young lady took us to the grocery store and purchased a good supply of groceries for us.

Rev. Bradley Wood Lock RMA 04-04-03 to 05-05-03

On that Friday we made our next move to Wood Lock. The shelter was one large room with partial bath, stool, and lab only. It had no cooking facilities likewise it had been left in horrible conditions, by the previous occupant. The wife, and I, cleaned it up, to livable conditions, and moved in. It was just good to have a place to hang our hat. The entire building only had four rooms in it and three of them were being used by the ministerial assn. And the fourth room was used to house people like us.

One of the rooms, on the ministerial side, was being used as a food pantry for needy people, and also for an office for the Wood Lock Ministerial Association.

Rev. Bradley, the Pastor and the head of the Ministerial Association was probably one of the most kindly, and caring individuals, that we ever met in our wanderings. Although he was limited somewhat, by his governing board, he gave us the key, to the food pantry, which allowed us to have access to all the food we wanted, including the frozen peaches. And I sure did make use of them. Since Wood Lock, was only ten miles or so south of Harriman, we continued to attend the church at Harriman.

By this time, Easter was upon us, and Rev. Bradley invited us to the Easter ceremonies, sponsored by his church, for the entire week before Easter.

This allowed us to have hot meals, at his expense, and some interaction with some of the other ministerial leaders, of Wood Lock. Unlike Rev. Bradley the other ministerial leaders were not sympathetic to our homeless problem, and begin to get rather nervous towards the end of our first ten day stay.

They did not like to have a stay of longer than 10 days, especially of one who would not work, or hold secular employment. Albeit with much reluctance, and with Rev. Bradley's good words about us, they extended our stay at least 3 times, with the explanation, that they would be unable to extend it further. Well! We had been there, and done that before, and knew that ultimately Gods will would be carried out no matter what.

One ministers wife who routinely helped out at the food pantry, became increasingly concerned about the wife, and I, feeling that we did not have the all around diet that we needed. She took it upon herself to buy us an additional amount of food, more she said to her liking. And again Rev. Bradley brought us a hot plate, and cooking utensils etc. for our continued occupancy. Fortunately the food pantry had a refrigerator.

Two interesting side notes

Wood Lock is railroad city, and the shelter was one block from several train tracks. Every hour on the hour, around the clock, one train after another would come screaming through town. Sometimes, one could even feel the vibrations, in the small apartment we were at. It reminded me of an old Lucy show, that I had watched, in earlier times, in which Lucy, and Ethel, along with their husbands, was vacationing, and at one point stayed in a one room motel similar to the one, we were staying in, near a train track. The movie went on to show Lucy's and Ethel's beds vibrating so hard, that is caused their beds, to roll down hill to the other side, of the room, because of the uneven floors, every time a train would come screaming through. Well our bed did not roll across the floor, but we felt sometimes that we might be shook out of bed. Comical: to say the least.

In as much as this shelter didn't have laundry facilities, we had been granted permission to do our laundry at the former Trinity Shelter for which we graciously accepted. One Wednesday evening, before church, we decided that we would take our wash to the shelter, but when arriving at the shelter, the manager, on duty was doing her own clothes, and realizing the time frame we had to do them in, she offered to handle the wash, enabling us to get to church on time.

When returning to the shelter, following church, for our clothes, we found out that our clothes, many of them new, had been burnt up in the dryer. The management was not the least bit happy, especially having to buy us some new clothes. That ended our laundry attempts there. We wondered where we might do laundry now, but we knew the Lord was in control.

Well as stated earlier, we continued to attend Harriman Church of God and on the following Sunday morning, following the clothes incident, while in Sunday School, the pastors wife came in, and handed me a note. It seemed as though the management of the shelter wanted to talk with us. We wondered what this could be about, in as much, as they had given us the cold shoulder, and told us not to come back, since the clothes incident. Waiting until after church we went to talk with them.

Upon doing so, they told of a man living in Union county, who had a residential home, for which he housed some mentally challenged individuals. This job, its seemed provided a house fully furnished, along with food, and salary. But by the time we arrived at the shelter, he had already return to his home in Union County. Management said: "it was right down our alley," and for all we knew, it could have been. So we decided to make contact with subject by phone. When learning of our interest he consented to make another trip, well in the access of 100 miles one way, to interview us. We met with him that same night, and agreed to help him out for a period of time. We knew we could not hold secular employment, but in this sense, we felt that this was ministry, in and of its self.

A short period of time before, I had received a vision of a beautiful house, and landscape, high upon some mountains with a city below but did not know what it meant. Albeit, as usual observed the prison gate being open.

When arriving at our place, Robert the owner discussed all of the particulars reference this new ministry. It seemed to be as the management had indicated, right down our alley. So we accepted it. By being involved with this, all of our living expenses would be paid, and in addition, we was to receive a $100.00 weekly salary, and in return the wife would do the cooking, and keep the wash done up, and keep the house clean.

Robert's Union County, Mt. View Plainview 05-05-03 to 08-26-03

We agreed to meet Robert in Clinton the next day. Early Monday morning we packed our meager belongings, and begin to make our way to Clinton a distance of near 45 miles, for the meeting with Robert.

In all of my fifty some years, I don't know, that I ever saw it rain harder than it did that day. See section on car, as, alluded to earlier, our car had a sun roof, which was off track, and would not close properly, and every time we turned a corner or went around a curve one of us would get wet. The electric window, on the driver's side was broke, and would continually fall down, inside the door, with no way to properly secure it. The defrosters was not adequately working, and to make matters worse the windshield wiper on the driver's side, was stripped out at its connection point and would only work when it wanted, which didn't seem to be that day. Fortunately we had an umbrella, for which we put up in the car, to help shield us from rain, but even with that we both were soaked to the gills, along with everything we had in the car, blankets, clothing, and what baggage we couldn't get in the trunk.

By the grace of God we continued toward Clinton, even though it seemed as all the powers of hell was against us.

After one of the most frustrating trips of our life we were finally able to meet Robert at Clinton as we agreed. I suppose to the public, and to Robert we looked like a couple of hobo's or stumble, bums, going to where ever.

We felt so embarrassed, for having to look the way we did, for surely, if he hadn't been in the need of help so bad, he no doubt would have told us to forget it.

After our rendezvous with Robert, at Clinton, we continued yet another sixty miles, or so, over seemingly, never ending mountainous roads, before turning on to this mountain road which was high above anything in the area.

When arriving at his place we found it to be a beautiful: ranch style home four bedrooms, with full basement, fully furnished, with nice furniture, over, looking the valley below, just as I had saw in the vision. Not to mention the fact that we were surrounded by mountains.

After having shown us around, he left us there alone, in order that we might get acclimated to our new surroundings. The following day, he brought the three individuals, from his elderly care center, in Clinton for us to watch.

Later in the evening, Robert's mother in law, to be, come to the residence, to explain the various procedures, we needed to follow, reference the occupants of his care facility.

As time progressed, we could see the reason he chose to go to a shelter to get help, as the wages he was offering, would not have been agreeable to any one, unless they were in the same precarious predicament, that we were in. From his own remarks, and from observation, we could see that he was hurting, for good stable help, and was obviously having to work his few employees, and relatives, way over the normal and expected time limits. This later proved to be to our advantage.

Having been in a similar environment, and working as a pastor, of a nursing home, I knew from time to time, that some of the individuals desired to smoke, and so before we accepted this assignment, we got a clear understanding, that no smoking would be allowed inside of the house.

However, the next day, when Robert's mother-in-law, to be came over to give us more instructions, she immediately started smoking. Being allergic to smoke as I am, I told her what the owner had said about smoking, in the house, and she in turn replied: "That he really didn't care one way or the other."

Finishing her cigarette, she left after having given us the needed instructions. Following her departure, I called Robert, and discussed with him the problems of smoke, and he concluded that it wasn't a problem, and that he would take care of it.

All seem to go fairly well through Thursday, albeit on Friday, Robert mother in law, to be showed up, to relieve us for our day off, and almost Immediately upon arrival, she lit another cigarette, and I immediately responded, that this was to be a smoke free environment.

She indicated that Robert did not mind, if she smoked in the house, nor did he care, if the elderly care patients smoked in the house. And she let it be known, that she would continue to smoke regardless of our feelings.

I again reminded her of what Robert had said, and she again reiterated her intentions to continue smoking.

At that moment, I told the wife, to go get our stuff packed, and we would leave this place, and I well meant it.

Immediately she relinquished her will to smoke in the house, complaining that smokers did not have any free rights any longer, and how unfair it was that she couldn't smoke where, or when, as she saw fit.

By some previous comments made, we knew that she had previously been working many long hours, as result of being unable, to find any suitable employees, and she knew all too well, that if we left, she would have to continue working long hours, by herself: as she was the one responsible for the welfare of these particular clients.

For the next month, everything went fairly well, and we continued to get our one day off each week, along with a minimal salary of 100.00 per week, and in addition, our housing, and all other necessities

Even this small amount of money seemed to be a lot when having not received any money for a long period of time.

Robert never did give us any set dates reference longevity of this job, but based on his comments, we felt sure that time was on our side.

By now, we had made contact with our friend Jeanie, whom we became personally acquainted with, while at the Mission in Knoxville. I had mentioned Jeanie's name to Robert in response to his plea for additional help, most specifically for our day off. With his approval, we made contact with Jeanie, and she consented to help us out, on the one day we had off, and Robert would continued to pay her as he did his mother-in-law.

With additional help things continued to run fairly smooth. In as much as Jeanie didn't have transportation, we normally made a trip to Knoxville, on Thursday, to pick her up, in order that she would be at our place, on Friday, and at times, she would continue her stay through Sunday, whereby giving her a chance to be in our Sunday Worship services, that I had established while at this elderly care center.

We continued our church services for them, on a regular basis, and the wife, through the day, would put on Christian tapes, the same as those that touched my life so dramatically, and this would always draw their attention.

Well the light seemed to show through. 1 Peter 2:9. From time to time she would see a couple of the elderly patients weeping, with tears, streaming down their faces, and upon asking why, they would reply: "Oh that beautiful music." God was doing a work in their lives that no one else could do. From time to time, they would ask her to play more of the tapes, and would beg, to stay up, even past their assigned bed times, just to hear the sound of the gospel music. See Amos 8:11

Two of the three clients, were elderly senior citizens, living out the final moments of their life, with poor health, in a strange environment, that they had not chosen, and I always will feel, and believe, that we was sent there, for that purpose, in as much, as it gave them a window of opportunity, to know the Love of Christ.

First time: to see the grandbabies since leaving our daughters house.

Feeling that we would be at this place for a good length of time, we made contact with the daughter. We was not sure of her reaction, in as much as she had asked us to leave, but felt sure, that she had been pressured, by the church, and in-laws, into making that demand, through the granddaughter. As it turned out, she was much surprised to hear from us, and the two grandsons, immediately wanted to come see us, even though it was in the access of 120 miles.

The following Saturday, they made the trip to our place, for the purpose of bringing the grandsons to see us. Even they, were surprised, to see the beautiful house, and surroundings for which, The Lord, had blessed us, with. Even though they had very little to say, the wife and I knew, that they were surprised to say the least. They simply could not understand how a man that would not work could afford such a place. 1 Corinthians 1:19

As stated earlier they, nor any one through the church, did not count ministry as work. After a fair length visit, they consented to leave the grand-sons there overnight giving the wife and I a good visit with them.

By now, a month had passed, and we were enjoying the ranch style house with all of the pleasantries, and amenities, but apparently, God had other plans. As I allude to earlier, we felt time was on our side, with perhaps, six months, to a year, but then on Monday, almost a month to the day, I awoke, to see the prison gate again. Would we be moving again? I mentioned it to the wife, and she discounted it, saying: "That she felt we would be staying for a long time." As the week progressed, the gate continually opened wider and wider, and on Friday morning, when I awoke the gate was totally opened. Ms. Jeanie, had stayed overnight, to enable her to be there on Friday morning, so that we could get an early start, on our day off.

The wife, and her was talking in the kitchen, and when I came out I said: Guess What?

Startled, they replied: What?

I said: "The prison gate is totally opened." They both were familiar with the meaning, and expressed their thoughts, that I might not be seeing what I thought I was seeing, and discounted it, and continued their conversation. Sure enough at 5:00 pm., that evening, following our return, Robert paid us a visit, and told us, that he had to discontinue the operations there.

He paid us for our weeks work, but immediately took the occupants to his other home.

Concerned about the short notice, I asked: "How much time we would have to find other housing?" He said: "That he would work with us, and give us time to find a place."

Well how does, one do that with no money in his pocket, in light of the fact, that we had received the commandment, not to express need'.

We knew that God had led us there, and that He would help us, but we could see no way out.

Since renewing our acquaintance with Jeanie, and she being familiar with our faith walk, had introduced us to a couple, at a small church in Knoxville, who as she said, was walking a faith walk, similar to ours. We begin to attend their services, as we could, consequently be coming good friends with the pastor and wife.

They turned out to be a very aspiring young couple, and very energetic for the Lord. As our friend had stated, they were walking a faith walk similar to what we were. For the next few weeks, we attended their routinely, as we felt lead. As we stated the church was in Knoxville, and we were living in Union County, right at 25 miles from the church. Seemingly when we would run short of gas money, The Lord would raise some one up to help us. By now, we begin to feel a command to go there on a regular basis. We became well acquainted with pastor and his wife, and on a couple occasions, he asked us to speak, for which we would always receive a love offering. By now another month had passed, and time was drawing near for us to be moving.

I didn't know how soon, but by now, Robert was pushing us to move, and at the same time, I felt that the Lord was severally testing us, reference to our obedience, of even going to that church, 25 miles one way, with next to no gas in our tank.

These were not normal roads, they were mountainous road, narrow, and very dangerous, and treacherous to say the least, but if, and when we did run out of gas, The Lord would always make sure, that we could get to a gas station. This probably happened from three to five times. On one given occasion we knew we had enough gas to get to church, but knew we did not have enough gas to get home. I had been asked to stand in for the pastor on that Wednesday evening, and so we had no choice but to go. He had told us, to keep the offering for our services. When arriving, only one other couple showed up at the start of services, but we continued our service as if we had a number of people present. When taking the offering, we only received a few coins, certainly not enough to get us any gas to get home on. The flesh wanted to think about our inability to get home, but God, had a message for me to give that night, and through His help, I was able to do that. But still yet I had that constant nagging in the back of my mind, how, would I get home?

We were near three fourths of the service when all of a sudden, one of the other members, and her son showed up, for the balance of the service. Immediately upon their arrival, the son came forward, and put in their offering of three dollars. What a relief! I now knew that we could make it home, for it was night, and I already alluded to the conditions of the roads in that area certainly no place to be driving gasless. Well that was on Wednesday, and on Thursday Robert paid us a visit, and really begin to press us hard to get out. I didn't know any more than he did, how we could move, for by now we had no money, the gas tank was next to empty, and we simply did not know what to do, but to pray. I didn't, and I couldn't confess need, and so I was unable to give him any suitable answer. We continued to pray, and standstill, which didn't make him too happy. We knew that from previous times, it had to be God, to give us the enabling power, to move. Later that same day, the pastor, had called to thank me for my help in the services, and ask me again, if I would handle the services the coming Sunday morning, as he again had to be out of town. I was reluctant to say yes, knowing the gas situation, but by now the relationship with The Lord had grown so strong, that for me to have said no, I believe that I would have greatly disappointed the Lord. How could I tell Him, I don't trust you Lord. Somehow I knew he would make away, although I had no earthly idea how that might be.

Having only three dollars to put into the gas tank that last Wednesday, I didn't know if I would even have enough gas, to get back to the church, much less home.

Well Friday came, and Robert was back to find out when we were moving. He was still unaware of our financial condition, and I wasn't interested in telling him. The balance of the week past fast, and now it was Sunday, and I knew that I had twenty miles to drive that morning to church, and I wondered if I would even get there.

In these times, The Lord always seemed to be so close.

As I was driving, I could look out the front, and rear windows, and literally see the Angels on the rear, and front bumpers, and riding as it were on the wings of the wind on both sides of the car, not to mention the fact that The Lord Jesus was always before my face, and at my right hand. See Acts 2:25: Spiritually speaking, one does not worry, when you observe this type thing. As we made our way toward church, that morning, I was reminded of the faith test, while still yet in the Pearl area, and somehow, I knew that God would take care of us, just as He did, all of the other times. As I was driving on the winding roads, and through the heavy traffic, God would whisper to me: "Just keep going, drive like you have got a full tank of gas, just keep going," and as I heard Him speak to me, I would in turn speak it to the wife, which encouraged her, as much as it did me. Through the flesh, I guess, at any moment, we would run out of gas, but it just kept going, how I didn't know, for it had to be on the Holy Spirits Power.

Well we made it to the church, without any problems, and I breathed a sigh of relief.

Well again, only one couple showed up for service, and they told us before the start of the service, that they had no money, for which to pay tithes, and so they bought us a pound of cheese, and a new bottle of dish detergent.

Well what would we do? I didn't know, only God, could help in this type situation. Old Slew Foot done his best to distract the best he could from the service, but failed miserably, for the service ended up being real good.

In the back of our mind, and through the flesh, we still had the nagging thought, about how we would make it home, but we knew, The Lord was in charge.

Following church, and the couple leaving, we locked the building, and headed for the car. I, was real sure, the car wouldn't start, for we had only put roughly two gallons of gas in it the previous Wednesday, before we had left Knoxville, and by now had driven right at forty to fifty miles, so I knew or at least I thought the car wouldn't even start. Much to my surprise, it started right up, and I headed for the closest gas station, thinking that I might find some money, but that didn't happen. I went inside the building, and talked with the manager, but that too ended with no results.

Well the wife, and I, headed for the wild blue yonder, up over the mountains. I drove two to three blocks from the gas station, and as we was passing the Executive Motel Inn, The Lord whispered to me: "You now are on me" Wow! And from that moment on, the car ran as good, as if it had 30 gallons of gas in it. The angels were so bright and visible as I stated previously. The Lord continually talked us through the entire trip, in the same manner as I stated earlier.

Knoxville is not without many stop lights, but we seemed to hit every one of them, on green, and we continued on our way, for near twenty five miles passing many stations, but it just kept going. As I alluded to earlier we lived at the top of a large mountain, and I had much doubt, and fear, as to whether, I would make it to the top, but as I turned on to the road, leading to our complex, the car continued on. I thought that any moment the thing would surely die, but it just kept going. I turned onto our road, and pulled in front of the house, in order to back into the drive way, and it died. It started back up, and I backed into the driveway, and shut it off. The Lord had given me this car many months ago, for proving time, and to my knowledge it had never run better than it did that day. I thought that perhaps, we had missed calculated the gas, and so we forgot about it, and went to enjoy another good home cooked meal, and rested for the afternoon. We prepared to go to church that night, but when trying to start the car, it would not start, it was dead bone dry.

That was the last test for this time, with that church, under that particular pastor. The pastor called from time to time, wondering why we never came again, but unwilling to express need, I was never able to give him a reason.

As I stated earlier, they were walking a faith walk, similar to ours, and was near ready to lose their house, for which the wife was getting extremely nervous. He had told me earlier, that he had been commanded not to hold secular employment, but at the wife's urging, he returned to work, so that he wouldn't lose the house. I later found out, that they had both been sick a lot, and since that time, I have not had any means for which to contact them. See Luke 9:62

Well for now the gas test seemed to be over, but now we had the housing problems to deal with again.

To refresh your memory, we had helped with the elderly for approximately one month and then Robert had chosen to end the care center, at this particular location, but said that he would work with us on housing.

By now it was the first of August, well past the time he felt we needed to find other housing, but he was not aware, of our circumstances although he should have been, in as much as he had come to a homeless shelter to find us, and not to mention the fact, that he had to give us gas money, in order for us to get to his place.

By now Robert was becoming fairly frustrated to say the least.

I believe that he thought we had reserves from which to draw from, but that was far from the truth. We had no money, no gas, and no way to move. Believe me we seem to be again at the Red Sea with no way out. He showed up practically every day, wanting to know when we were leaving. Yet, I was unable to tell him anything, for we didn't know ourselves. I couldn't tell him, that he had been unfair, for now we had lived there might near two months, since he had moved the elderly residents out. But how would we be delivered.

By now we had made friends with a neighbor boy, next door, who was involved with a Christian music group, and I begin to communicate with him. I had mentioned to him about my car not running, although I was quite positive it was out of gas, I was not sure, inasmuch as it had run so good, the last time that I had driven it. He offered to look at it, having some knowledge about vehicles. Having tried to start it, he believed along with me, that it was just out of gas. He offered to take me to the gas station, just down the mountain, and I told him, that I didn't have any money at the time, for which to buy gas, upon finding that out, he said: "I do" and then he went and purchased me five gallons of gas. Well at least by now, we had a partial way to proceed. A short time later Robert showed up with his girl friend, demanding that we move out. His girl friend was not as polite as he was, and already being mad, over the smoking incident, said that if we didn't move, they would throw us out, and lock the door. Having been involved with the Real Estate business and having been involved with the two evictions alluded to earlier, I said: "You can't do that." His girl friend went crazy, and started making all kinds of threats.

Robert spoke up and said: "We don't want to go that way, but we need the house." He then began to press me, for the reason, that I was not moving.

Not really knowing what to say, I said, "If you want me out that bad, file for an eviction." For I knew, that I would have at least an additional 20 to 30 days before we would have to be out by court order. He asked me why I felt that way, and I responded, and told him the truth. While he continued to talk with me, his girl friend went out, and called someone on the cell phone, I assumed to be the Sheriffs dept. for which I am sure they confirmed to her, the same thing, that I had already told them. Knowing that his girlfriend was beside herself, and very agitated, he went out to the car, to calm her down, and I suppose, for some discussion, as to what she found out from the Sheriff's dept. Shortly thereafter he came back into the house, by himself, and asked me, how much would, it take, for me to move. We settled on $200.00, with that, he said: "That he would be down to the house early the next day." Likewise, we were true to our words, and we started packing our meager possessions. When arriving, he gave us the $200.00 for which I offered, to return to him, but by now he seem to be sympathetic to our need. So with that, we ended our stay Aug. 26. 2003. One would ask why we went this way, but it always seemed that nothing of an answer would come until we had done all we could to stand see Ephesians 6:13.

PEARL TN. in RV 08-26-03 to 09-02-03

We returned to our old stomping ground, Pearl County, hoping for something good to happen. With the $200.00 in our pocket, we had a bit of freedom. First on our agenda, was to find housing. At the west edge of Pearl City, on St. Rd 72, we found a station which rented RV's. For some reason, I felt prompted to stop, and talk to him, about one. The prices were far above anything that we could afford, for any length of time, but the management, did consent, that if we kept the RV on his property, and not take it on the road, that we could stay in the RV for one week, for a $100.00. Somehow, the daughter, and son-in-law, found out that we was living, in the area, and paid us a visit. They wanted us to keep the grandbabies for a few days, but we refused, in as much, as we were living in such cramped housing, "a thirty two ft. RV., Does not leave one, with much room." Likewise, we was living next door to the office of the RV rental place, and we felt that they would be, none too happy, with that arrangement, in as much as we had not made any arrangements for other then the wife, and I.

Well the week passed by fast, and we still had no plans to proceed. We knew, that The Lord would make a way, as He always had done, since being in this walk, but as of yet, He, had not made His plans known to us. We knew, that we had to be out of the RV by Tuesday, and so we continued to seek, His will for our lives. We was just down the road from The New Beginning Church, where I was the former assistant pastor, but knew that we would not be welcome there, so we attended somewhere else, for a little peace, and spiritual encouragement. Well Monday, came and went as usual, and by Tuesday, we still had not received any answer, and we decided that we would return to The Inn of Lenoir City.

Lenoir City, TN. Inn 09-02-03 to 09-04-03

With some negotiations, with the manager, and The Lord being very much in control we were able to obtain a room, for an additional three nights. It was always a joy to stay at this motel especially after having lived in an RV for a week.

After we moved to Tennessee, in the RV., alluded to earlier, I had no desire to own another house, but an RV., only. But, The Lord reminded me many times, that no matter how elaborate of an RV., one has, it will never suffice for a house. Over and over, we have found that to be true. It is just not the same. Well we enjoyed the hot baths, and the comforts of this good motel, for the next three days, not to mention the air conditioning, for by now, the weather was hot, humid, and sticky, if you know what I mean.

Our time was nearing, to the end of our stay at the motel, and our money was all but gone, and our options, seemed to be very limited. We had always had a place to stay, but now, it seemed to be different. There seemed to be nothing, forth coming, when all of a sudden, the wife spoke up and said, "You know, we have been tested, and tried in every other way, but as of yet, we have not had to sleep in the car." "It may be that The Lord is trying to tell us something." Well as much as I didn't want to agree with her, the remarks that she had made, resonated well, within my spirit, and brought to remembrance the many stories, that I had heard over the years, of other ministers doing the same thing. By now, it was 2:00 PM., and check out time had arrived, and we loaded our few possessions into the car, and left. Much prayer, and discussion occurred that day, of what we might do, but we knew, The Lord was in control, and that He would lead and guide us every step of the way.

OUR NEW SHELTER

In Car 09-05-03 to 09-10-03

As stated earlier, the weather was hot, and muggy, and heavy with mosquitoes, and every other type of bug one could name.

For the record, I was not keen on having too subject, the wife, or myself for that matter, to this type of environment, but we seemed, to have little choice.

For the balance of the next few days, we meandered, around town, taking advantage, of various parks, one with a small creek, and various self serve service stations which had cooking facilities, enabling us, to have hot meals, etc. Fortunately we had much canned soup, cereal, snacks, and coffee on hand. Late in the evening, we headed to the main city park, for which we knew, would be well populated with sports fans, and joggers etc.

Near midnight, everything would quite down, giving us a chance, to sleep. The park was routinely patrolled, giving us, a more secure area to stay in. On occasion, the police would stop by, to see if we were ok. We had much time on our hands, and the wife, and I, would use this time to sing, praise choruses, that by now, we were so use too. The presence of God, was so surreal in this time of despair, to the point, that the both of us, found ourselves rejoicing, singing, and laughing, more then what we had, for a long time. For some unknown reason, "God," a nice, breeze begin to flow, and the temperature, would moderate to comfortable conditions, causing us both, to enjoy the surroundings. It brought back to remembrance, the times that I use to camp out.

At one point, a mosquito started to bug us, and I rebuked it, in the name of "The Lord Jesus," and from that time on we had no bug problems.

Another time, the wife felt a bit threatened, by a carload of Hispanics, as I went to the bathroom, approximate 400Ft., from where we were parked, but as I returned to the car, they left, perhaps seeing the Angelic visitation that I see continually.

There was a walking path, near where we parked. Many would come out early in the morning, just to walk, and sometimes, we would get out, and walk our selves. On next to the last night, we spent in the car, a middle aged lady, who routinely used the walking facilities, came to the car, following her walk, in the morning, asking us, if everything was all right. She stated: "That she had noticed us there for the past several days, and wondered if she could be of help." I stepped out of the car, and begin to strike up a conversation with her, informing her, of the fact, that I was a minister. She begin to share with the wife, and I, some of the problems, she was going through, giving me a chance to witness to her. She left there, to use her own words, "blessed," with the promise, that she would be back later. That was 7AM., and that evening, at 9:00 PM., she, and her son brought all kinds of snacks, hot chicken, and sodas, etc. and gave us $20.00, for which we were very grateful, as our gas tank, was getting low. She stated: "That help would be coming."

The next day, while we were at another park, with the water front, alluded to earlier, the police came by, and notified us, to get in touch with the Local Ministerial Association.

Lenoir City Inn 09-10-03 to 09-13-03

When contacting the Ministerial Association, they gave us a check for $100.00, and a 40.00 gift certificate, at Jerald's restaurant, and housed us again, at The Inn of Lenoir City, for three more nights, and with part of the money, we had received, I was able to get a fourth night. Having been in the car for five nights, it was nice to again, enjoy the luxury of a motel, with the hot baths, and comfortable surroundings.

By now, we had come through Hell, and high water, and our relationship was stronger than ever with the Lord, and likewise the wife and I had a stronger relationship. We both wondered, what would come next, following our four day stay, but again we knew that The Lord was in control. For by now we had learned to live from day to day. Matthew 6:34 We well understood the true meaning of the song.

I DON'T KNOW ABOUT TOMORROW

1. I don't know about tomorrow, I just live from day to day, I don't barrow from its sunshine, for its skies may turn to gray. I don't worry o'er the future, for I know what Jesus said, And to today I'll walk beside Him, for He knows what is ahead.

2. Ev'ry step is getting brighter, as the golden stairs I climb: ev'ry burden's getting lighter: every cloud is silver lined. There the sun is always shining, there no tear will dim the eye, at the ending of the rainbow. Where the mountains touch the sky.

3. I don't know about tomorrow, it may bring me poverty: but the One who feeds the sparrow. Is the one who stands by me and the path that be my portion. May be through the flame or flood, but His presence goes before me. And I'm covered with His blood.

Chorus—Many things about tomorrow. I don't seem to understand; but I know who holds tomorrow, and I know who holds my hand.

Well time passed by swiftly,

Wilkerson's RV 09-13-03 to 09-19-03

On Sept. 13, near check out time, a minister by the name of Frank Wilkerson, having learned of our plight of homelessness, through the Ministerial Association, met with us at the motel.

Being greatly concerned, He wanted to know how he could help us. Immediately he offered to find us a job, and housing, for which he would have been well able to do, in as much, as he was well known in the community, and had a lot of influence.

Following his proposal, I told him, of my divine ordered faith walk, and the commandment that I had received, reference full time ministry with no secular employment.

He responded: "I don't understand that, as I have worked 10 to 12 hrs daily, and then preached to midnight many times." He said: "I have done that all my life." He seriously questioned that command, but stopped short of saying, that he didn't believe me. He then asked me: "What I had done wrong, in my life that I wanted to punish myself in such a manner." He just couldn't understand, the reasoning behind it, and didn't agree with me in any sense.

He did not believe that his parishioners would be willing to help us under such conditions, unless I would be willing to go to work fulltime. I responded: "I am sorry, but I can't do that."

Still concerned, he stated, that he had a RV., which was similar to the one that we had just moved out of, and said that we could use it, for a week. On that Saturday, after having made arrangements with the RV park: he granted us permission to drive it to the Knights Inn RV., Park, approximately 20 miles. It was not far from where we had stayed, in the other RV., and not more than a mile from the church for which we had been asked to resign.

He stated: "That the Ministerial Association, was doing what it could, to find us housing, but was having problems in doing so, in as much, as we could, but would not, hold secular employment." He concluded:

"That he had done all he could, because of our stance, and instructed us to stay in contact with the ministerial association," and so we did.

The following Friday, we received a call from Rev. Wilkerson

Telling, us that the Ministerial Association, had found us a place to live in Knoxville, and advised us to contact them. Upon doing so, the secretary stated;

"That we needed to go to The Charity House, in Knoxville, TN. as quick as possible.

With that in mind, we returned the RV, to Rev. Wilkerson, and again headed for The Charity House.

CHARITY HOUSE

09-19-03 to 12-01-03

Upon arriving at the facility, we found that it was owned and operated by the Holly Charities. They had renovated a, unused wing at The Mercy Hospital, to house various individuals at age 55 yrs. and older, who needed temporary housing, for whatever cause. We seemed to fit the criteria for this temporary shelter.

The operators of this shelter, was the same organization that owned the Trinity shelter in Harriman where we had stayed 37 days in February.

If they had been able to cross reference our name with the Harriman shelter, this housing would have been blocked, But I believe, The Lord had his hand on the situation, and they never found out about it until the exact timing of the Lord.

When arriving at the Charity House, we were met by a well caring lady Rita who seemed to be in charge of everything. She immediately assigned us a room, and then took us to the dining room, for a hot meal. That remained our home thru Dec. 1. 2003. The rules were somewhat repressive, in that we had to be inside the facilities by 10 pm. The wife was able to interact, with many of the elderly people there that were entrusted to the facilities care, while their younger siblings, whom they lived with, worked outside of the home. At night, they would leave, and return to their sibling's home. Albeit: there was an estimate, 10-15 other individuals that were homeless, like we were. Even though it was a religious organization, the atmosphere was severally suppressed, so far as any religious activity. Even the television was controlled by the people instead of the facility, which resulted in less than a Holy atmosphere. The management did not care to keep control of the television, so far as programming was concerned, which resulted in all types of filthy and dirty programming continually being watched. Being the church facility that it was, one would have thought, that they would have controlled it better.

This particular facility was almost like a small city, having many conveniences of a small city, and with that I was able to meander about the facility having many opportunities, to pray, and witness with people. Likewise it had a prayer chapel which enabled me to have as it were, a prayer closet.

The facility likewise was in close proximity to various business districts in the North Knoxville area, enabling the wife and I to visit them from time to time. I have always enjoyed living in the city, and so I was able to spend most of my time meandering about the city while the wife spent many meaningful moments with the elderly people brought in during the day.

Rita the main manager was very sympathetic, to our cause, and having explained to her my conviction, and feelings reference secular employment, she did not feel it necessary to push me into any employment, but didn't know how long, her boss would consent to such an arrangement, in as much as all of the homeless occupants were suppose to be seeking employment.

From time to time questionnaires were handed out, to each individual to explain their attempts at finding employment, but obviously my questionnaire, did not come into the hands of anyone knowledgeable about my circumstance. Perhaps it was divinely hid, until the appropriate time. Rita's manager John was quite aggressive and would have acted upon the problem at once, had he known, but that didn't seem to be the case. Well time continued on.

In the mean time, I came into contact with a little church down the hill from the facility, and I was able to minister there on occasion.

In addition, the church for which we had formerly been connected with, while at Robert's had come under new leadership. Now called THE NEW LOVE IN GOD:

One of the former parishioners, which was under the former leadership, stated that it was not the same. Never the less, I felt prompted to go to it. The pastor, and his wife, seemed to be caring, but didn't hesitate a bit, if he, or some of his few members needed a smoke break, he would promptly call a halt to the service, and go outdoors, and smoke. That was something, I couldn't live with. In times past, I didn't even allow my son-in-law, to be connected to our ministry as long as he smoked. And I certainly was not in favor of continuing our attendance there, nor being connected in any way with the operation. Not to mention, my wife's stance, for which is just as strong, if not stronger than mine. But I kept feeling prompted, to continue my attendance at the church. To make matters worse, I felt, I needed to be there every time the church doors were opened, which was Sunday, and Tuesdays, and Thursday, for prayer meeting. The wife didn't agree at all, and was fairly belligerent with me about going.

My wife has always been more apt to attend services, then what I have been, but this time she was different. She did not want to set under a cigarette sucking preacher, any more then what I did, and one time, the only time in our marriage, that I can remember, she refused to go. The Lord continued to remind me: "That he was not going to ask me about the pastors smoking, all he was going to ask me about, was what I did to obey him."

Well this thing continued on past October, and into November, and now Thanksgiving, and Christmas Time.

By this time, the facility, we were living at, had scheduled a Halloween party, for the occupants, of our shelter, and the head Priest, and his entrusted friend Julia, who was over the management at our facility, was to be there for that party. I told the wife: "That if she came, she would recognize us from Trinity shelter and that we would be as good as finished there. Even though the Head Priest showed up, Julia did not show up that night, I believe, because of the Lord. For he had his perfect timing, knowing that if she did show up, our time would have been finished at this facility.

John the head administrator of our facility, and Rita's boss was not happy that we would not hold secular employment. He just could not understand the reasoning behind it all. Obviously he had not shared his feeling with Julia his boss, for she no doubt would have recognized our name.

We could see John's irritation growing against us because I was not busily engaged in secular employment. And he finally forced Rita even though she was in tears, to give me an ultimatum, go work, or be out of the facility, by mid December.

Because of the continual enabling power of The Lord that I saw at work in my life, reference His command of no secular employment, I told John, that if he would stick a gun to my head, threatening me with death, if I didn't go to work, I would tell him to pull the trigger.

He was so stunned, by the remark, that he just glared at me, in disbelief, and seemed to be at a loss for words, for a few moments and then reiterated his statement, that I would be moving as he had stated, if I did not comply.

In the mean time, the wife had become close with one of the caretakers, as a minister wife, and from time to time, this lady would share with her, some of the problems she was going through. The caretaker greatly respected her, for her belief and trust in The Lord.

She had indicated to the wife, that she could be fired, if it was made known, that she had been sharing her problems with her. Albeit, one evening, near 9:00 PM. The wife, received a call on the residence phone, and it was from this care taker. She ask "if she could come to the parking lot, and talk," Startled, she consented. When going to the parking lot, to meet with her, she began to poor her heart out to the wife. Fortunately the wife was in position to minister to her.

At the close of their meeting the wife, had prayer with her, and she returned to the facility. The following day, while on duty, as she passed the wife, in the hall, she grabbed her hand, and handed her a $100.00 bill. My God is good. Just in time for the Christmas Holidays.

Well by now, Thanksgiving was just around the corner, and management had given me, to 12-15-03 to get a job, or I would be forced to move. In as much as it was Christmas time, and having received the money, mentioned earlier, the wife, and I, walked down the hill, to a small shopping center, to look around, and to do a bit of shopping. Having accomplished that, we headed back to the shelter, and on the way back to the shelter, a woman, jumped out of her car, and ran up the hill, to meet us, saying that, "The Lord had sent her there to prophesy, to some one, and she was sure it was us." As she begin to talk, we told her, of our faith walk, and the loss of our children, and grandbabies, as result of the faith walk, and I shall never forget the prophesy, she gave us that night. She said: "The Lord would cause all of our grandbabies, and children, to look up to us, for what we had done, and that we, would not stand before them ashamed." My! What a powerful prophecy, for a time, when the wife, and I, seemed to be at our lowest ebb. We were nearing Christmas, and among many people, yet alienated from our children, and grandbabies, whom: we loved dearly, because of innuendo, circulated by, and from the church people, and supposedly good friends.

I never will forget the look on that young ladies face, as she told us the prophecy The Lord had given her.

Shortly after that, I was walking in the parking lot, and came across a gift certificate, from the American Buffet, for which we used for our Christmas dinner.

Well by now the firestorm was becoming stronger than ever, over having to attend the church that I earlier described. For I just couldn't see why, I would be commanded to go to a church such as that.

In one of the services, that I attended, I followed the pastor outdoors, and, as he was starting to smoke, I gave him a very strong rebuke for standing in the pulpit, and then smoking. It did not seem to bother him a bit, and he made the "lop" sided excuse: well I don't believe it will keep me out of heaven.

I said with a half sarcastic remark: "I am not so sure," and went back inside. Was I God? I must have thought I was. See Psalms 1

Well time, begin to dwindle down towards our moving date, and again we was unsure, as to where we might end up. By now, the wife, and I, had become a custom to this much moving and realized that our future was very much in The Lord's hands.

The wife, and I, continued to have much discussion about the church, and with the exception of the one night, that she refused to go with me, she continued to go with me to the service even though she did not want too. The Lord continually reminded me of his former conversation with me reference the church.

On Friday, 11-28-03 following a nice Thanksgiving, Julia the head administrator, paid a surprise visit to the facility, in as much as she couldn't be there, for the Halloween Party, to take care of some general business.

While there, she just happened to pass the wife, in the hallway and abruptly stopped her, in the hall, and said: "Don't I know you from somewhere?" The wife being startled, reminded her, of our stay at Harriman, earlier in the year. At about the same time, seeing what was happening, I walked up, and she immediately begin to question me, as to why we still was not working with Robert, at his elderly care center. No explanation would satisfy her, and with that I went downstairs.

As indicated earlier we had been given to 12-15-03 to move. Having finished my business downstairs, I started to enter the elevator, to return to the floor our residence was on, and immediately was confronted by Rita, with tears in her eyes, telling me, that I had to be out of the facility 12-01-03. Julia with a cocking grin, and smug look on her face stood at a short distance to see if Rita followed her orders.

Well that gave us three days to find a place, in a city that we were unfamiliar with. Just what would we do? And where would we go? This abrupt move caused quite a bit of concern, but we knew that God was in control.

On Sunday 11-30-03 following the morning service, I had transported a friend to his apartment, in the Knoxville area, and while doing so, the door glass, on drivers side, fell down inside the door, and when trying to retrieve it, I shattered the entire glass. By the time church time came, that evening, and even though, I had been commanded to go every service, I told the wife that we would not be going that night, because of the glass, in as much, as it was, extremely cold, windy, half rain, and sleet, and at times snow. I also knew that we had to move the following day, and I just wanted to get prepared the best I could for that. Albeit: the wife for some reason wanted to. To make matters worse, she was very insistent about going. After a round of words, I appeased her by going.

I had mentioned earlier, to the Pastor, that we might be moving shortly, but the last time that I had talked with him, l did not know when. Now it had all changed. Well, as always, we arrived at the church, 15 minutes or so, ahead of starting time, and as usual went and sat down, and Bro. Raymond came to us, and asked, if we had found a place.

I said: "No." He said: "Come to the back, so we can talk."

Anxious to find out what he wanted, we went to the back room. When doing so, he showed us the two back rooms, of the church, which were currently not being used.

He said that he, and his wife, had been discussing our situation and felt to offer them to us for a time, until we could find more suitable housing.

The one room used as a Sunday school room, already had a couch and TV in it. And the office, which was never used, already had a microwave oven, and a coffee maker, along with a refrigerator, and he offered to bring his new queen size bed for us to sleep on.

Wow! We couldn't believe it. Now I knew why The Lord had sent us there. On Monday we moved all of our meager belongings into the two rooms at the rear of the church.

Bro. Raymond 12-01-03 to 01-18-04

Little did we know what was ahead, had we known we might not have taken the place. But for the time being it sufficed. I have often wondered, what would have happened, had we not obeyed the Lord. We would not have been able to return to The Rescue mission other than in the general section, forcing us to be separated, for which, The Lord had protected us from. But now, because of our obedience, we had a place to go. Thanks to The Lord which never fails. What few church members they had, welcomed us. In addition, I was asked to preach on various occasions. I was surprised that he would even ask me to preach, after my wrath on him, for his smoking.

By now our remaining funds, begin to rapidly disappear, leaving us without the ability to buy gas, or food.

In as much, as the refrigerator had a small ice compartment, I had to make a trip daily, to the gas station, for ice.

Within the next week, we were able to use our gift certificate that we had found, in the parking lot at The Charity House, for American Buffet, just a few blocks from the church.

Within the next few days, having looked at our food supplies, and seeing that we were near out, Bro. Raymond brought some food over to the apartment, for us to eat.

The last service, before Christmas, they took up a love offering for us, giving us chance to buy a small amount of groceries.

By the end of Christmas, we totally ran out of food, causing us to go on a God ordained fast, with nothing more than complements IE., Catsup, mayonnaise, mustard, relish, etc., for which the wife would not eat. This fast was quite grievous' to her, causing her to have much hunger pangs, but God saw her thru.

THE SONG THROUGH IT ALL the song comes to mind.

1. I've many years in sorrows, I've have questioned for tomorrow there've been times I didn't know right from wrong: But in every situation God gave blessed consolation that my trials come to only make me strong.

2. I've been to lots of places, and I've seen a lot of faces, there've been times I felt so all alone: but in my lonely hours, yes, those precious lonely hours, Jesus let me know that I was His own.

3. I thank God for the mountains and I thank Him for the valleys, I thank Him for the storms, He brought me through; For if I've never had a problem I would not know that He could solve them. I'd never know what faith in God could do.

Chorus Through it all, Through it all, I've learn to trust in Jesus, I've learned to trust in God; through it all, through all, I've learned to depend upon His Word.

By now, the church was in discussion, about having a dinner, following THE NEW YEAR service. And let me tell you, the wife, and I, was all for it, in as much as neither one of us, had ate anything, for a solid week.
And when it did come, I don't mind to tell you, that we both pigged out.
Shortly afterwards, the wife and I, were in the sanctuary, using the PA system, (we had obtained permission from the pastor) to sing, and praise God, something, that we had been doing, on a routine basis. We used this as a way to keep our minds off of the many problems.

VISION THE WHITE STALLION AND JESUS

On this given day, as we were singing, very spirited, I was looking up into the left hand corner of church, for no reason, and all of a sudden "The Lord Jesus Christ," came crashing through the walls, on "His White Stallion," with what appeared to be, a sword in His mouth.) of that church, sending the blocks, and wood flying, everywhere, and no sooner, did I see him crashing through the walls, then He, was directly in front of me. All: seemingly happened, within a micro-second. By the wife's words, my countenance changed immediately, and I started crying. The wife, ask me what the problem was, and, I said: "You are not going to believe what I just saw." For the wife, hadn't seen anything. This was an experience that I shall never forget. Well I believe God was preparing me for what would happen shortly.
For the next few days, everything went fairly smooth, and routine. All of the parishioners, along with Bro. Raymond, and his wife, seemed to be at ease with the fact, that the wife and I were occupying the back two rooms of the church.
Albeit, we knew that they were having severe financial problems, mainly

142

because of the escalating heat bills and our occupancy made a bit of difference, in as much, as the heat needed to be kept at a higher level.

While we maintained occupancy there, the wife, took the opportunity to keep the church clean, and I did some general repair on the windows, and other areas, that was poorly insulated, which caused the heat bills to soar. Albeit: that did not seem to alleviate the heat problems.

They expressed their appreciation many times, for us being there, to help them out. As time began to dwindle on, we could see the handwriting, as it were on the wall that our moving time was drawing close, although they had never mentioned it. Not to mention the fact that they seemingly sought to keep us at ease.

Shortly after we had moved to this location, and in as much as the wife is an avid reader, helping her to keep her mind off of the many problems, associated with this type walk, we had established our residence, at this location, through the post office, enabling the wife to get books from the local library.

On Friday, 01-16-04 both the pastor, and his wife, came to talk with us saying: "that they were concerned, that we had no income, little or no food, and support." As he begin to talk, he pulled out a list of food banks, for which we could get free food, and also furnished us with the name of his attorney, who he said, could get us social security disability, as he had, all free of charge.

Following his presentation, I told him of my conviction not to confess need, by going to the food banks, and certainly was not interested at that time to get disability, as it would stymie my ministerial: aspirations in the future.

He reiterated that this would cause no problems for me being in the ministry, for I could accept money under the table, as he did. I further indicated that if I had to start depending on this type help, then I had better quit trusting The Lord and go to work. I had been at this juncture many times, and I wasn't willing to bow now, any more so, then I did earlier.

His countenance changed immediately. He, and his wife, just couldn't understand why we would feel that way, and they immediately, left.

Approximately two, or three hours later, he was back, saying that he was going to have to, ask us to move. He later admitted, to thinking that I was a wanted man, because I did not want to confess need.

I said to him:, "How long do I have?" I felt, that he would be willing, to give me some space, in time.

He stated: "That he would give us, till Friday 01-23-04, to be out."

I asked: "If I might stay till the following Tuesday 01-27-04, which would give me might near two weeks, to find a place."

He wanted to know why, I needed more time. I explained to him, that it seemed to be more difficult to move Friday, through Monday.

He was reluctant, but agreed. We visited some, and he left. Later that afternoon, he came back, asking for more explanation, as to why, I needed more time. I reiterated, my previous stance but he just couldn't understand it, and left.

Well night time came, and the wife, and I, retired as usual, but continued to be very restless. We knew we had to move, but had no earthly idea where, not to mention the fact, that our gas tank, was on empty, and no cash, for which to buy any gas. He had promised us the extra time, to move, and so we promptly dismissed any problems, and went to sleep.

As usual, we awoke Saturday morning, and ate breakfast, and set down to watch the news at about 8:00 am, and we heard someone loudly pounding on the door. We turned the alarm off, and opened the door, and much to our surprise, there stood Bro. Raymond, and two large teenage boys with boxes. I ask Bro. Raymond what was going on, and he sharply and abruptly replied, get your stuff, and get out. We got the boxes here, and he immediately told the boys, to start boxing our stuff, and carrying it out.

I encountered, saying: "That we had an agreement that we could stay till 1-27-04.

He abruptly replied: "I want you out today, and we came to move you out today. "Your, a wanted man, and you are going to jail."

Knowing the law, I said: "You can't do that,"

He got right in my face, and said: "Don't you cause me any problems, or I will take you down. Don't cross me." He continued his demands to the boys, to get our belongings, and throw us out. I attempted to talk to him, but he started shouting, half wildly: "Get away from me!, Don't touch me! Don't come near me! You are going to jail!, and he ran across the street, to the parking lot on the south side of the building, as if he thought, I was going to do him harm. I really think, he thought, that I would do something, to harm him, or the boys.

I saw, that he was determined to throw us out, and I told the wife, by now frantic: "Slow down, I have got to get to a phone, to call the police." The two teenage boys, not use to dealing with this type problem, and having been left alone with us, was running around like chickens without their heads, trying to follow their orders. I kept telling the wife: "Slow down packing, and slow the boys down, for they were determined to follow Bro. Raymond's orders to the T.

His first threat of me going to jail, startled me to say the least, and I must admit, that I was a bit nervous, but then all of a sudden, I begin to think, why would I go to jail, I hadn't done anything wrong, and I availed myself of the opportunity to run across the street, to the medical center, to call the police, trying to make sure, that Bro. Raymond nor the boys would see me, for I wasn't sure, what they had in mind, not to mention the fact, I didn't like leaving the wife alone, with the rage he was in.

When calling the police, the dispatcher asked: "The problem and I explained it to him, as fast as I could." He asked, if I had established residence there, and I answered in the affirmative. He immediately sent an officer out. When the police showed up: Bro. Raymond come running back across the street, to find out the problem. She immediately asked both of us, for our ID's, and then wanted to know the problem. If I ever saw a lying preacher, it was that day. And all the demons of hell, was doing what they could, to intensify the problem. The issue at stake, had I established residency. Having been satisfied that I had, the police lady immediately responded to Bro. Raymond, saying, you can't throw him out like this. You have to give him a notice, and go through the general eviction proceedings, for which I knew all along. He begin to tell her how unfair, I had been, and how he needed the office, we was using, and every other fabrication, that he could think of, almost to the point, of being ridiculous. But none of his lame excuses seemed to make any difference or any sense to the officer, and she again, reiterated her former comments, based upon the law. That is, he could not throw us out on the street, as he intended, and for which he would have done, if I had not been able to get to a phone. One of the most ridiculous things, he said to the officer, was: "Well I was going to give him a hundred dollars, to help him on his way." Well he lied about that, and many other things, for I could readily assure you, that I would have gladly left with a $100.00 in my pocket, but that was far from the truth. As I stated, it was even questionable, if I had enough gas to get to the station.

Following the officers comments, he told the boys, which by now had loaded the couch, and the television, to go to the truck. I asked the officer, If they could return the couch, and television, but she refused, and she did not enforce my request. We were fortunate that they had not had time to get to the bed, refrigerator, and microwave, along with the miscellaneous dishes.

After the boys went to the truck, he stated to the officer, that he wanted me to sign a paper, saying, that I would be out the coming Tuesday, a week earlier, then what he had previously given me.

The police lady ask me: "If I would be willing to do that under the conditions, since it was a church,"

I consented, that I would, if he did not cause me any more trouble. At his request, it was put in writing, and I, and Bro. Raymond signed it, in front of the officer.

Following the form being signed, he stated to the officer, that he didn't want the wife, and I, to attend their Sunday morning service. He wanted us to leave, and come back after church, I did not agree to that, for I knew all too well, that had we left, he would have locked us out, and changed the burglar alarm code, and we would have been out on the street, with not even our personal belongings. The police lady was in full agreement with us, and could not understand why he would make such a request being a minister. She asked him his reasoning for such a demand and being unable to answer her, she told him, how silly his request was.

I asked Bro. Raymond in front of the police lady for copy of the moving date, that I had signed, and he refused to sign a second copy. Taking note of his refusal to sign another form, she stated to me, that she would make note of it on the police report, so that if there would be any more trouble, I could refer back to it. With that, Bro Raymond and the teenage boys left.

By now it was near 11:00 am, on Saturday, and we knew that we dare not set foot off of the property, for had we done so, we would have been locked out. Thank goodness, for my real estate management training. So with this in mind, the wife and I, set as it were, in prison, without a TV. Or, a couch, and so not knowing anything else to do, we turned on the mikes and begin to sing. The darkness and the blackness of hell seemed to be there, but as we begin to sing our praise choruses the area lightened up.

I SHALL NOT BE MOVED

1. I shall not be, I shall not be moved, I shall not be, I shall not be moved, Just like a tree planted by the waters I shall not be moved.

2. Jesus is my savior, I shall not be moved, Jesus is my savior I shall not be moved, Just like a tree planted by the waters I shall not be moved.

Over and over that day, we had the feeling, that he was watching the building, just hoping that we would leave, but we was smarter than that. We continued our occupancy that night, being very leery, praying, and praising, The Lord, trying to keep our minds off of the day's events. Perhaps this was one of the worst storms that we had ever gone through. We couldn't help but wonder what would happen tomorrow. Sunday services was just hours away. Would Bro. Raymond or any of the parishioners show up? Would they cause more trouble?

The devil continued to permeate, and torment our minds, with them nagging thoughts and questions. And yet seemingly we were powerless to do anything about it. No gas and no money. We would have gladly left, and shook the dust off of our feet, but unfortunately that wasn't an option. Well one hour, seems like ten hours, especially when all seems to be going wrong, and today was no different.

Sunday morning came, with little or no rest for either one of us, for we both were on pins and needles as it were. As stated earlier, we did not know what to expect.

We awoke at the normal time and with little appetite, ate little breakfast, and waited, for Sunday morning service time 9:30 am. I had told the wife, to finish packing, for we did not know, what to expect. I would have gladly discussed it with him, but that was not an option we had. The church building set on a corner lot, with large windows in the front, enabling us to see what was going on, outside. Every now and then, we would see him circle the block, like a shark waiting for the kill. And from time to time, I would step out doors to see if I could see him, and sure enough he was setting in a vacant lot, a half block down the street, just waiting for what we didn't know. Church time came, and no one showed up. Had he canceled? These nagging questions, kept us on edge, and it seemed the devil was doing a good job at keeping us on edge. I knew that we had the law on our side, but in earlier conversation, he had admitted at being a mountain man, and further stated that some of the mountain people would not hesitate to shoot you, for the least cause. Well we didn't know, but I can assure you, we did a lot of praying. The wife, and I, both would have gladly left that place, but that wasn't an option.

For some reason, about 1:00 pm he must have thought that we left the building, for he very quietly came in the front door, and started to tip toe back towards our living quarters. As it was, we was setting just inside the front door, not readily visible, from his vantage point.

I said; Well Bro. Raymond, did you come to talk? You would have thought that we shot him in the foot, for he jumped forward, turned around, and quickly departed from the building, not saying a word.

Time continued on going slower than ever, and with not knowing what to expect, we continued to pray, and sing, and discuss the events. From time to time, I would step outside to see, if I could see him, and his whereabouts, and for the most part, found him setting in the same vacant lot as before.

It seemed that every demonic force in Hell, was playing this thing for all it was worth.

We wondered if they would cancel the evening service as they did the morning service. Only God knew.

Thus far, I had out foxed him at his own game, not by my choice, for I didn't have any other option.

Near 3:00 PM., from our advantage point, I could see part of the side parking lot, and it looked as if: there were a couple of vehicles in it.

I stepped out to see what was going on, and found there to be another pastor, who I had meant earlier, seemingly a very polite individual, talking with Bro. Raymond, along with another couple, and a gentlemen in a wheel chair. They begin to head for the front door. I went back inside, and told the wife, and we both went back into our living quarters, not wanting to cause any problems. They all came into the sanctuary, and the topic of discussion, was the wife and I. Wanting to desperately work something out, I came into the sanctuary, where they were, and headed toward Bro. Raymond, to talk with him.

He began to scream: "Get away from me! Get away from me!, Don't talk to me!, The police is coming!, The police is coming!

I immediately encountered his remarks with: what have I done?

I made reference to the $100.00, that he had told the police he offered me, and then I said: "If you had offered me that amount of money, I would have been long gone, but that was far from the truth." Why did you lie?

The lady that was pushing the man in the wheel chair, immediately encountered with: What do you mean, trying to get money out him?

I said: "I wasn't trying to get money out of him I was only reminding him of what he told the police earlier. He is the one that said that, not me."

She continued the argument, why should he give you a 100.00? She said: "You can go to the mission about 10 blocks away, and it won't cost you anything to stay."

I reminded her again, that I was not trying to get money out him, nor was I trying to cause problems. It was him, that made the agreement for my length of stay, and not, ourselves. The other pastor, begin to respond, well the police is on their way, and you are going to be moving. I told him about the agreement that we had made, in front of the police lady, giving me till Tuesday to leave. And then I asked Bro. Raymond, for the copy of the agreement that we had signed. He immediately responded, what agreement? There was no agreement. By now, I believe this pastor begin to see the light, as I begin to share with him, some of the things that went on. He asked: "Why, I had mentioned the money, and I reiterated the facts to him, that had he offered me, the one hundred dollars, as he had told the police, I would have been long gone, but I was unable to leave, because of having no gas and/or money, and was taking Bro. Raymond's word, that I could stay till Tuesday. By now, he was rather sympathetic to our need, and said, he wished he could help us, but was not financially able, and neither did he want to get involved with the squabble.

While I was talking to this pastor, the lady had left caring for man in the wheel chair, and was chiding with my wife, saying; "She was the one paying rent, and she wanted us out of there." No explanation from the wife would satisfy her, and she became rather assertive, that we leave.

Well by now, an officer had arrived on the scene, and he came storming in the back of the church, demanding who it was, that would not leave. And I replied it was me. He stated: "You are going to get your stuff, and get it out now or you are going to go to jail."

I said:, I can do that, but I have got some questions." And then I went, on to tell him about the signed agreement, for which Bro. Raymond had consented to the day earlier, in front of the police.

I also told him, that he needed to talk to his supervisor, for according to the law, they had to go through eviction proceedings, because of me establishing residence.

He apparently had some previous experience with this type of problem, because he did as I suggested, and stepped outdoors, to call his superior.

I followed him outdoors, and told him about the remarks Bro. Raymond had made, reference the $100.00, and he felt that in as much as I was bringing it up, that I was trying to extort money out of Bro. Raymond. The remarks did not make him very happy. I assured him that I was not trying to extort money out of Bro. Raymond but reminding him of what he had said.

I pressed him, to let me talk with his superior, but he would not let me do so, and continued to discuss the problems, with his superior, almost to the point of arguing.

By now, a second officer, had arrived on the scene, and ask the officer on the phone, if he needed help in the eviction. Much to my surprise, the officer said, No! We can't evict him, because of him having established residence.

Following the conversation, with his superior, he returned, to talk with Bro. Raymond and the other parishioners, on the inside, leaving me, and the other officer standing outdoors.

As he begin to tell Bro. Raymond and the others of the outcome, he alluded to the possibility, that if they would go to the court house, which was opened till 5:00 PM., they might possibly be able to persuade the judge to take out a warrant on me, for extortion, in as much as I said, I would be willing to leave for $100.00.

That was a misquote for I had only told the officer what Bro. Raymond had said, he would do, in front of the lady officer, on Saturday.

All the while, the wife was inside listening to the conversation of the officer, to the parishioners. She came running out the back door of the church, where I was talking to the other officer, saying: "There getting ready to file a warrant against us, for trespass, and extortion, and holding the place for money." By this time, the other officer had come outside, and begin to talk with the same officer as I was, and seconds later, Bro. Raymond came out the back door hallowing, I have got your $100.00, and I went over to talk with him, and to get it, He said: "You will get it just as soon as you leave."

With that, both officers threw their hands up, and left. They certainly couldn't understand anymore then what we did, for the devil, had set a trap for us, but it all backfired.

150

It seems that the man in the wheel chair had more compassion then the rest, and did not want to follow through with the officer's suggestion therefore he gave Bro. Raymond the 100.00 for us.

Still talking with Bro. Raymond, I said: "I at least need to go get some gas before anything, and I asked the other pastor who by now had already taken another $10.00 up from some other source, to go with me."

I wanted all of Bro. Raymond remarks, and his actions along with all of my action to be viewed by this pastor for by now I would not have trusted Bro. Raymond as far as I could throw him.

I wasn't sure I would even make it, to the station. The first thing the pastor did when getting into the car, was to check the gas gauge, and he expressed with astonishment, you was not lying was you!

Well the car loped all the way, to the station, just verily making it. As I had stated, I well knew the car was nearly out of gas.

While I was getting gas, the wife continued to pack the remainder of our items, and we put them in the car, and shook the dust off of our feet from that place.

Before I left, following him handing me the $110.00, I tried to shake hands with Bro. Raymond, but he would have nothing to do with me, and followed me to the door, and told us in front of the other pastor, that if we ever set foot on his property again he would have us arrested for trespass. True colors were shown that night.

Well we had been thrust out seemingly, as the children of Israel, from Egypt, and we didn't intentionally barrow anything, as the children of Israel had done, but in the mass confusion, mayhem, and turmoil of the last two days, we accidentally packed one of his wife's sheets, and a teaspoon for which we had no intentions of doing.

Hopefully someday we will be able to return those items without threat of arrest.

"In the shadow of his hand hath he hid me. "Isaiah 49:2

Well by the time this incident was over, we were ready for the sack for we had literally treaded upon the, the lion, the adders, and dragons as Psalms 91 says. Not a very comfortable position to be in. Thank God for His Ever abiding love for which He watches over His children.

Executive Inn 01-18-04

Well we were not sure where we would spend the night, but with a $110.00 in our pocket, we didn't need to worry, about where we would sleep.

Our first stop was to the Executive Inn Motel, in Knoxville. Checking with the office, we found it to be, out of our price range, so we opted to go on down the road further south, for a cheaper place, but the further we went, the dirtier, and the more costly they became, so we finally returned to Executive inn. Following our registration, at the Executive Inn we treated ourselves to a nice fish n more dinner at Long John Silver. If we ever earned a dinner, it was that night.

Well I must confess I didn't know what God had in mind but stood on Mt. 6:33. God had never failed to date, and I knew well that He wouldn't fail me now.

Inn of Lenoir City 01-19-20-04

Following a good night's rest, we headed back to our old stomping grounds, Pearl County, and back to the Inn of Lenoir City. We made arrangement, to stay for two nights, so that we could check out the ground as it were, but it was as if, we were returning to Egypt, void of any immediate, or futuristic plans, so far as housing etc. except we bow to mortal man. Things seemed to be as dead as ever, and all of our old contacts, were seemingly indifferent to us, and our needs. When I say needs, most everyone, that we were acquainted with, and knew, in the area was highly aware, of our needs, and the plight, that we was in, but by now, they, had become indifferent because, we would not bow to their mortal plans of going to work, at a secular job. The normal expectation, but we were not in a normal situation.

Psalms 37:25 says, I have never saw the righteous forsaken, and his seed begging bread,

As before we did not confess need or went as it were begging for bread. By now, we had come to realize that God was our provider, and not man, and by now we had seen God: raise up one person, after another, to provide for us, in a perfect and timely manner.

Spiritually speaking who worries under them conditions.

We even inquired about some apartments, in the area, but all seemed to be dead to us, and all the doors were shut. Well God: What do we do now? We had been at this junction many times, and knew that God was leading and directing. As I have stated many times, I believe that one of the main reasons, we had been thrust into this faith walk, was to bring us to full realization, of Gods' continual provision, no matter what circumstance you might face. And by now we had faced many crisis's, but have found God to be more then faithful in every situation. And this time was no different, then before.

While at the Charity House place Rita the manager, because of her over all concern, for the wife, and I, had given us a couple of places, within the Knoxville area that we could check with, reference housing, for which we hadn't done yet. So the next morning, after all avenues of escape had been checked out, we headed back to Knoxville, to see what we could do in that area. By now we were running out of places to go. As always, we did have the option of returning to the mission, to stay at night only, but that was not an option, as the wife, and I, would have been separated at night. And either, one of us wanted that, and thus far The Lord had always honored our feelings.

FAMILY INN, KNOXVILLE, MERCHANTS DRIVE, 01-21-04, SUPPLIED BY LIFE OF ABUNDANCE CHURCH

When arriving at Knoxville, we made contact with the places whose name we have been given, but found only one place that was receptive to us. As always, they questioned us, as to why we were in the predicament that we were in, and we explained to them the reason. Like all the rest, they didn't agree with us on our faith walk, but consented, to give us a one night stay, at the Family Inn, not to mention, another lecture on the ethics of work. If I never received another benefit from this faith walk, at least, I could boast of the fact, that I now knew better than anyone else, about the ethics of work, in as much as I had been lectured at every stop along the way.

Since receiving only one night at this Inn, we had no other option, but to head west, unless we wanted to stay at the Rescue mission, and I had already alluded to that earlier. At the time, we didn't have the means, to make any long distance phone calls, to the Crossville area, for which we had learned of two shelters.

Fortunately, there was an elderly care taker at the Family Inn, who helped us get placed in the room, and likewise allowed us to use his cell phone. Well The Lord always makes a way, where there is no way.

FAMILY TOGETHER SHELTER

01-22-04 TO 03-31-04

Our first call was made to the Family Together Shelter in Crossville, TN. I was able to talk with a Mr. Dollar owner, and operator, of the shelter, and he confirmed, that he had room for us to stay. At the time, we did not try the other shelter, for we had learned through Mr. Dollar that they would not allow the husband, and wife, to stay together.

After a restful night, we awoke early in the morning, and made the long trip to Crossville, nearly 65 to 70 miles, over some of the most mountainous terrain in the state.

The car, seem to run without any problems, as we continued our trek over the rough terrain. While on the trip, we crossed into a different time zone, and arrived an hour earlier than our appointment.

When arriving at our destination, we had a long talk with Mr. Dollar and found him to be rather sympathetic, with our plight, and, he was highly interested in the fact, that I was a minister, and stated that he felt privileged to have a minister staying in his shelter.

We seem to bond, if you will immediately, and for the balance of our time there, the wife and I, begin to help him in various capacities around the shelter.

My primary work was in administrative and running errands for him mostly in our car, for which he paid for the gas. The wife did the cooking, for which he enjoyed tremendously, and supervised the cleaning activity at the shelter.

This man had such a unique, loving, helpful, and caring attitude, to all concerned, no matter what predicament one was in. His love, for his fellow man, seemed to transcend, all barriers, no matter how far one had fallen.

Mr. Dollar was a retired x-cop from New Jersey, and having been trained to handle the most brutal, and dangerous type individuals, he stated that: "He had been so harden by his work, and so severally sadden, at the results, that he now chose, to turn his life around, to help individuals in need.

I ask him his motives for doing this type work, and he said: "That he just wanted to repay The Lord Jesus for being so good to him." He was a Lutheran, and the beauty of his life, shown through, for his love, for The Lord Jesus Christ, and for his fellow brethren.

The first Sunday we were there, he asked if I would go to church with him, and so, the wife, and I, even though we were Pentecostal, chose to go with him to the church. I was surprised at the service, for I very much felt the hand of God in the services. Even though we were among people, with great means, we were treated well, and not looked down upon, or belittled in any manner.

01-25-04 HAD HEART PROBLEM.

Following service, we returned to the shelter, and the wife prepared dinner, for all of the residents.

Shortly after dinner, I begin to have a severe hurting in my chest. We had received a light snow earlier, and I had shoveled the snow off of the walk much the same, as I did at any other time, but for some reason, I couldn't get rid of the pain in, and around my heart. As the afternoon continued on, I became increasingly concerned, about the pain that I was experiencing, almost, as a dart going through my heart. After several hours, the word got to Mr. Dollar, and he gave the directive, to have me transported, by ambulance, to the emergency room.

I detest this type thing with a purple passion, but I was in no condition to argue, so I went, realizing, that I didn't have any insurance. I had earlier been diagnosed with heart problems while at the mission in Knoxville, TN., but I had given little thought to it, now, It, came back, to me to haunt me. After much routine treatment, and test, they dismissed me by the end of the day, for I was feeling no pain, because of the extensive medication. No determination was made as to why the pain. Primarily: because I was uninsured.

By now the wife was beginning to panic, and was being pressured by the social workers, to apply for TENN CARE and all of the other compliments of the state, such as food stamps, etc. I had not felt any release to do so, because of the Lord's command, for me, not to confess need, and so I still, was very much in opposition, to filing for this help. I could have done so many times, but said I would rely on The Lord, and we continued our trust in the Lord. Psalms 91

Thank goodness, for a wife, that was willing to go along with me, and the faith walk. She had been called upon many times, to walk this way, and she, like me, was willing to do the will of God. Many marriages have been put on the rocks because of such a radical walk, but she has always been willing to do His will, even more so then me. Thank God for her spiritual strength, and faithfulness.

We continued our attendance at The Lutheran Church, for about one month, and then, I begin to feel a tug in my heart, to continue my search, for The International Holiness Church that I knew, had been established in this area, by a Rev. Albert Woods a brother-in-law to the Rev. Steele who had introduced me to Pentecostalism. I alluded to him earlier, in the forepart of this book. For some reason, I seemed to be unable to locate the church. After a month, I finally did locate the church, and the wife, and I, decided to visit it.

As I alluded to earlier, I was ordained with the International Holiness Church however, my license had expired, and with no funding, I was unable to renew them. But now, I thought it possible that I might get them renewed since this was a CH Church.

So on the Sunday we decided to attend the Rev. Woods Church in Crossville. Rev. Woods was surprised to see us. He alluded to a conversation that he had just had, within the last week, with his Brother-in Law David Steele, as to the whereabouts of Bill Paige. And now as he said: "We came meandering into his church from nowhere." He couldn't believe it, and treated us fairly well. He was well aware of everything that had happened in Pearl City, but had very little to say about it. At the conclusion of the service, he asked the wife, and I, if there was anything that he could do for us, and I stated; "That I would like to get my license active again" and he offered to help, but that never came about.

For the next few weeks, we continued to go there, and were asked one time to teach a Sunday school class but beyond that, nothing happened. The wife and I, have often wondered, why The Lord wanted us to go there, for there seemed to be nothing good, that came out of it.

A short time after beginning to attend that church, Rev. Woods ask the wife, and I, if we cared, if he would divulge our whereabouts to the daughter. She still was attending the New Beginning Church at Pearl City and according to the Rev. Steele pastor of church she was in much distress in as much, as we had not stayed in contact with her. We had, not had any contact with her, for the past several months, since being at Robert's and for the most part, was fairly frustrated, at their attitudes, toward us, over the faith walk. We did not give him, the permission to tell of our where about.

Till now, they didn't seem to care, one way or the other, and I guess, we just felt like letting then stew for awhile. That came as some surprise to him, but never the less, he abided by our decision.

Well for the next few weeks, we continued our work, at the mission, and from time to time, Mr. Dollar would send people to me for counseling. The assistance manager of the shelter at this time, who normally was in charge when Mr. Dollar was not on site, became quite frustrated, that I now seemed to have, as much authority as she did, and she decided to just leave. This made the, way for I, and the wife to be in charge, while Mr. Dollar was away. We would always keep him informed, of any difficulties, that we felt would affect him or the shelter.

While there, I had the privilege of praying for a number of people and from time, to time, I would lead them in a confessional prayer, and only God knows where those prayers ended up.

One time in particular, an elderly gentleman, John Anderson who was living at the shelter, was a confessed alcoholic, and was not bashful about telling anyone. One day: while discussing with him, his plight of homelessness. I asked him very bluntly John Anderson how did you get to this position in life at your age? He was in his mid sixties, and poor health.

He said: "I can't get my ID., without my driver's license, and my driver's license without an ID. Consequently I can't get any form of help. The official ID. was put out by the drivers license bureau.

Almost immediately after he said that, The Holy Spirit illuminated me, and I called him back into the office, and ask him: Did you not tell me that you just got out of jail, before you came to the shelter?

He answered; "Yes."

I said: Don't you have an intake form from the jail showing that you were incarcerated?

He said: "Yes." And I told him, to get it. With that, he dug it out, of his few personal belongings, and while he was doing that, I called the Jail, and asked them, if the intake form from the jail would be sufficient documentation, to get help, and they stated: "yes." As soon as he produced his intake form, I immediately took him to the Drivers License Bureau, and got his ID issued by them, and then took him to human resource center, where he was able to get a generous monthly allotment of food stamps. And later I tried to help him get Social Security. Unfortunately, he was unable to stay off of the bottle long enough to get it. For years, this man had been running the streets, of every city, in the area, hungry, with little housing, i.e. even confessed to buying mouthwash, and seeing a patrol car, approaching, would take a drink of it, and then start intentionally, staggering, as if he was drunk, so that he could have a place to stay at night. What a plight to be in! No money, no food, no shelter, few clothes, to even keep himself warm, and with little, or no concern, from no one, to even try to help. He was a no body. Few people, would realize, what it is like to be in that predicament, but I believe, The Lord took us this way, so that we would know, just what it was like, in order that we might be able to help some poor, lost, and dying soul, and last but not least, to point them to the way of the Cross. I think so much about Jesus' words, Matthew 25:42-45 I hungry and you fed me not, I was naked and you clothed me not,

If one could just see the pain of the poor, hurting, lost, and dying souls, not to mention the hard hearted church officials, that makes it might next to near impossible, to get help. It, dear friends would rend, your heart, if you have a love for Jesus.

Another gentleman in his 40's hurt by a divorce, and forced into homelessness, just couldn't believe it, because the wife, and I, offered him a Pepsi. He was very bitter, and resentful, especially to anyone that called themselves Christians, for as he said, and I came to know, might near all homeless shelters are basically funded, by faith based groups, and churches, that proclaim to be Christians.

He told of how he had stayed in one shelter in the Chicago area around Christmas the year before, and on Christmas day, he along with all of the other people were kicked out of the shelter, following breakfast, and given a sack lunch, for dinner, and told not to return to the shelter until supper time, which was around 5:30 pm. He spent Christmas day, in the park, wrapped in a blanket, in knee deep snow. Everything being closed, he had no, where to go. He also told of many times of having to sleep under a bridge, in the cold, with no one caring. If one would like to see religious-osity, and hypocrisy, at its best, I would invite you, to go with me, to some of the many shelters that we have seen, and been in.

But thanks be to God, the shelter that we was in now, was not that way, for the owner Mr. Dollar had a heart for the people, even at his own expense, as our stories will prove out.

Well by now, our car was past its going stage, and one day, while on an errand for Mr. Dollar, on behalf of a resident, at the shelter, my alternator, locked up, shutting my engine down. The shelter was located next to a mechanical garage, so when returning to the area of the shelter, I stopped at the garage, for information about repair, of our alternator. Telling the mechanic on duty, the year and make of our car, he stated: "That I would be lucky to even find a alternator, and if he did, it would cost in the excess of Two-hundred dollars," but gave little hope.

Well, that was our way around, but I knew, that I couldn't afford that type of expense, so I had determined not to worry about it.

Not to mention the fact that I was still under commandment, not to confess need. As result, I did not say anything to anyone about it. How albeit, the gentleman, that I was transporting, at the time, immediately went into the office, of the shelter, while I was attending to some other business, and told Mr. Dollar of the problem. He immediately attempted to contact me, but found that I was out of the shelter at the time, and so he summonsed, the wife, to the office to find out the problem. At the time, she wasn't aware of the problem, or as to the expense, of the problem, and so she was unable to answer any of his questions. With that in mind, he told her to have me contact him as soon as I returned. When arriving back at the shelter, she told me immediately, of the urgency of his need, to speak to me. When going to his office, he asked rather abruptly, and directly, the problem with my car. Not wanting to express need, I tried to sidestep the question, but he was very short, and to the point. Finally I told him. He immediately gave me the orders, to get the car to the shop next door. The estimate was near $250.00, for which he paid for, out of his funding. At the same time, the window on the driver's door mentioned earlier was missing, and he wanted me to have it fixed, but no glass could be found for this age of car.

Well little did I know, that his funding for the shelter, was running out, but he begin to share with me, the problems he was having, reference keeping the shelter opened. The doctor, who owned the building to the right of the shelter, had recently purchased the shelter building also, and had doubled the rent, forcing Mr. Dollar to run out of funding. It seemed that all doors were closed for keeping the shelter open. By now, the governing board, for the shelter, was beginning to grow lax in their drive, to help Mr. Dollar. When learning of an upcoming board meeting, I inquired of the reason for the board meeting, and he informed me, that if something wasn't done at this meeting, he would have no other option, but to close the shelter, by the end of the month. He asked me to set in on the meeting, and to give some suggestions, but unfortunately, no suggestion, or funding was available.

I arranged for TV Channel 10 news, out of Knoxville, TN., to come and visit the shelter, and to air their findings, and the need for this shelter, but even that didn't seem to help

As stated earlier, there was another shelter by the name of Living Life: in the area, which was continually supported by the area's aristocratic churches, and the high minded politicians within the local political arena. They showed little care, or concern, for the, mission's objectives, nor the unfortunate individuals who was forced to live in this arena. No amount of coaxing or explanation could convince them of the need for a second shelter.

One interesting side note from the TV, interview, was that the wife, and I, was seen on Television, by the daughter, and she got her prayers answered by knowing where we were at, and finally made phone contact with us.

For our remaining days at the Family Together Shelter, we tried every conceivable thing going, to make the thing float, but all to no avail. While there, I had become highly involved, with the operation, and management of the shelter, and if you remember, in the earlier part of the book, The Lord gave me instructions, to observe every operation and it seems that The Lord gave me the privilege of doing just that.

I believe that at some point in time, I will through our ministry, have a shelter. I have learned much, while I was there, for which I believe, will be beneficial to me in the future.

Time began to dwindle down, faster, than what I wanted it to, for again, we had no earthly idea, where we might end up. As stated earlier, that I had been informed, by many, that the other shelter, Living Life would not allow husband, and wife, to stay together. In as much, as that was the case, we did not feel that this was an option for us.

Toward the end of the month, I begin to assist, Mr. Dollar in securing the remaining individuals, a place to stay, through The Living Life. By now, the population had dwindled down, to five men, plus the wife and I. There seemed to be a lot of friction, based upon innuendo, between the Living Life shelter and The Family Together Shelter. There seemed to be major problems for them, to even accept the men, from Family Together Shelter. They declined at first, but somehow, the thing came to the attention of the appropriate city officials, and we later had a visit, by the president of the board, for The Living Life saying: "that they would take them." By the time we got the necessary records in place, we were right up, to next to the last day, to be in service.

All of the individuals at The Family Together Shelter kept asking me: What are you going to do? Where are you going? I didn't have the slightest clue, but I kept quoting Mt. 6:33 over and over. Well to say the least, they thought like everyone else, that I, and the wife, was crazy. But God was still alive, and well, on planet earth, and He, and He alone, was in control. Towards the end, of next to the last day, I took the remaining men, over to The Living Life Shelter, by now only two, because of the missions tough legalistic standards.

They all were familiar, with their tough Christian, legalistic, attitudes filled with, hypocrisy, seemly full of dead men's bones, as it were, just as the scriptures quote, with little or no care, for any one, most of all, the homeless. To them, they were a bunch of "no bodies," and that is the way that they treated them. As earlier stated, they were supported by all of the high dollar churches, in the county, many of which did not want to put up with the down and out people. This became a well known fact. The entire operation, seemed to be governed, by high dollar people, who could have cared less, about the poor man, or the homeless state, he was in. They had what they called, "a hands up policy, and not a hands out policy." And they followed that motto to the tee. The founder of the operation, in the beginning, I believe, had a sincere desire for this work, but now, it was taken over, by a bunch of societal aristocrats, who could have cared less. Without impunity, or without any concern for the welfare of an individual, they would kick a person out of the shelter, for the slightest infraction.

What would drive a homeless man to the point of sleeping behind a service station, in the cold, of dead winter, and then end up freezing to death, as opposed to going to a warm shelter. The rigid rules, and regulations, that the mission embraced, seemed to be more than the general individual could stand.

The long, dead dry church services, that each individual, was required to attend, seem to play against the very nature of one's mind, body, and soul. Even me, and I am a minister. If they could have just showed some love, it would have gone a long way, but that was far from the truth.

LIVING LIFE WED

03-31-04 to TUES. 04-27-04

I escorted the men to the shelter, accompanied by their records. All of the men rebelled, about going, but they had no other choice. They needed a place to stay.

When arriving, I asked to speak to the owner, and his wife stated: "That he was not there." I then introduced myself, and handed her the records of all the men. As the discussion continued for longer then I wanted, I stated that I needed to get going, as I had to find me a place to live.

She encountered: Do you not have a place to live?

I said: "No, we have to move also." She asked me: Why I didn't ask them for a place?

I replied, That, I was married, and that I did not want to be separated from my wife, and so I chose, not to seek shelter there for that purpose.

She stated, that I needed to talk with her husband, as they did have a place contrary to what I had been told, and told me, to come back in a couple of hours, and discuss it with him.

When returning to the facility, he began to question me some, as to why I was homeless. He was a minister himself, and so I shared with him, my conviction of not holding secular employment. He like all the rest disagreed but seemed to be more sympathetic to my need then I first thought he would be. He took me to one of the houses, on the premises, and showed me a three room apt at the back of it. Surprised! I said: "I was told you wouldn't house husband and wife together."

He replied: "That is not entirely true." He went on to say, that I could move into the apt yet the same day. Knowing their stance on the hands up and not hands out policy, I again asked him, if it would cause any problems for me not holding secular employment.

He stated: "No," and told me to move in. I then raised the question with him about me attending his church, vs. the one that I had specifically been told by The Lord to go to, and he agreed that there would be no problems.

With all of the questions seemingly answered, I returned to The Family Together Shelter, to move all of our meager possessions to the apt. Having moved in, we were summoned to the office, to fill out the necessary registration forms.

After getting settled in our new surroundings, I approached the owner, about helping him in the office, as I did with Mr. Dollar, for which he was aware of, and the wife helping in the kitchen.

He shouted, "You are not going to help me in this office, and I don't need no help, in the kitchen." I also expressed my interest in helping him in the chapel, but again he refused, and stated: "That I would have to have ministerial credentials, and furthermore If, I did, it would have to be approved by the board.

My continued discussion with him, seemingly made things worse, as he had already obviously determined in his mind, that I, nor the wife, was fit to be connected in any way to his shelter. We were, "no bodies."

He then, began to question me, as to why, I did not hold secular employment, and wanted to know all the details about the church that I was connected with, and as to why, they wouldn't help me, and seemingly a million other questions, for which I didn't care to answer.

He was a former Pentecostal, reformed Baptist, and began to discuss theology with me, reference the two churches, for which I declined to get involved with, and with that, another supporter went down the drain.

Reference his remarks, about my credentials, I contacted Rev. Woods, pastor of the church, I was attending, and he said that he would assist me in having them renewed. I informed the owner of the shelter, of the promised help, and told him, Rev. Woods would be in contact with him.

Shortly thereafter, I asked the manager, if the Rev. Woods had contacted him, and he indicated that he had made contact with him, but that he didn't give me a very good report. Likewise the owner/manager, shared with our new friends, for which I will introduce shortly, obviously telling them much of the innuendo that he had pickup from who knows where.

When finding out about the whole thing, I went back to Rev. Woods, and told him what the manager, had stated, and he denied having said anything derogatory about me, only God knows the truth.

The Lord later gave me a scripture reference the incident See 1 Cor. 1:19

The men's shelter is located in the basement of the church, and the office, dining room, and women's shelter, occupies what use be the parsonage.

Our residence was next door, being a two unit apt. house, and we, was living in the rear apt. At this time we were the only couple living on this particular premise.

We were prohibited from using the cooking facilities in our apt. which forced us to go to the dining room for our meals.

Dining Facilities

The, Facilities had an average of 15 to 25 men and women, for which they served meals to on a daily basis, morning, noon and evening.

Jeanie was in charge of the entire dining area, including cooking, and likewise headed up the food bank. She steadfastly refused to prepare any hot meals, for the people in the morning, even though there seemed to be plenty of things to fix.

The only thing that she would serve was pastries, cereal, and half cold coffee. On one occasion, even the milk was tainted, by being outdated.

From time to time, various churches were involved with helping to fix the meals on weekends, and evenings, Thank goodness for that, on behalf of the homeless.

The main thing that concerned me was that these men and women were expected to get out, and go to work on this type food, in the rain, snow, sleet, it made no difference.

Board of Health regulations seemed to not be in effect. Health inspections seemed to be at a standstill.

Out dated milk, pastries, not fresh enough to sell in the stores, and meat, was picked up, from various stores, for use in the shelter.

Smoking was allowed in and around the food bank, causing much of the smoke to waffle in and around dining facilities. Diabetic residents were required to give themselves shots within one foot of the food distribution area, The women who lived in the shelter, was allowed to run shoeless in the dining, and cooking areas.

None of these infractions made for good dining, or good health benefits.

The waste was unbelievable.

In our residence, the refrigerator was used for storage, for the main dining, and cooking area. And on the day we moved in we found 11 gallons of out dated milk, for which we had to throw away.

Four flats of strawberries, had been stored in the refrigerator, and obviously had been forgotten. Out of concern, that they would not go to waste the wife cleaned them, and took them to the dining room, but to our knowledge they were never used for the occupants of the shelter.

An abundant amount of donated clothing and other misc. items were continually being donated to the shelter, with little or no care given to the preservation of them, nor were they being distributed to anyone.

This shelter had the potential for being a great place for housing the homeless, etc. but do, to poor management, to many chiefs, unqualified help, poor health standards, and an over abundance of waste, not to mention their tough legalistic standards, both secular, and religious, made for a very poor shelter. We found this to be one of the worst shelters we were in.

To make matters worse, the two men that I had help transfer from the Family Together shelter were all gone, kicked out for whatever, and to make matters worse, the owner would always come to me, and tell me about it, as if I could do anything about it.

In the end, I never did make any achievements with James Brady for in his eyes, I guess, we were just stumble bums, looking for a free ride.

OUR NEW FRIENDS AND OUR CONNECTION

Rev. George and Bonnie Green and Robert and Linda Cook

As it turned out, both couples had left Baltimore MA., under similar conditions, as we had left our home. Just as Abraham had left his surroundings, likewise our new friends had done the same thing. Get you up, and go for a land for which I will show you. At the time of our meeting the wife, nor I was not aware of their walk, and neither were they aware of our walk.

We was not sure, where this particular segment of this faith walk would lead, but we did know, that it could not continue as it had, For every book in God's Word, screams out (life). Let me tell you, Life is not living in the homeless shelters, moving, and roving, from one place to another, in hopes of finding a place to hang your hat. I believe that God was using us, in many ways, some of which I, alluded to earlier, and this was just another tool, to bring me, to a position in my life, where he wanted me to be. I also believe that there are seasons in one's life, for testing, and training, but as a permanent life style, it goes against everything the Bible teaches. I felt very much, that we were at the end of this particular segment of training, and sure enough, and unknown to us at the time, we were ready to meet out God given and divine connection. We had run out of places to go, in this area, and if for some reason we had not been liberated from this type walk, we would have been required to go into the Nashville area near two hundred miles to the west. We were not sure how we would be liberated, but we did know that God is faithful to all of His promises.

This from the very start was a God given connection, for which no one could have done, but God. It is interesting to note, that there was approximately a three week window of opportunity, for us to have met. Had that been delayed for some reason, such as disobedience etc. we would not have met. Faith, Love, and obedience wrapped in a garment Praise has always been the name of the game, since we have been doing this, and I am sure, it was the same for them.

By now we had been at the Living Life Shelter approximately two weeks, and one day as we was leaving the dining room, following dinner, there were two ladies helping out with some various chores, in the dining area.

Rev. Bradey, and his wife, the owners were nowhere around, and with a little more freedom them usual, because of their absence, we tarried in the dining room for a short while, just talking to various ones, and for some reason, whether by accident, or providentially, I just happened to mention James Delbar's name and the one lady which we now know to be Miss Linda hollowed out in her loud booming voice: "Oh Yah, that's my man." Because of that, we struck up a short conversation, with them that day. Later I told the wife, when I got back to the apt. I was going to find out, who these two ladies were, for some reason unknown to me, they stood out among anybody that I knew, especially the ones that day.

Shortly after we had met the two ladies, in the dining room, the wife begin to have trouble with two molars, that had re-grown in her mouth, at least 20 years, after she had all of her teeth extracted, and was now wearing dentures. The last two years, from time to time these molars became bothersome to her, causing her much pain, but would shortly go away, however this time, the pain persisted. One day, during that same period of time, while I was visiting the office of the former Family Together Shelter, Mr. Dollar ask me how the wife was doing, and I replied, that she was having some trouble with her teeth. He was always appreciative, of the work, that the wife and I had done, and continually showed concern for the both of us. When telling him of the severe tooth ache, he immediately called his dentist, and got an immediate appointment with him, at his expense. Within an hour, she had the molars out, and we counted it as another blessing. When returning to the Living Life, and being in much pain, she asked Jeanie and the other kitchen help, if she could have some soft things to eat, but they made no effort to do so. Another example of their indifference towards the no bodies. When the two ladies found out about the problem, they immediately purchased some soft items for her to eat.

For the remaining days, that we were at this shelter, I would watch for them, and every time, I saw them come to the premises, I would make a point to talk with them. Shortly after our initial meeting, while in the dining area, while Mrs. Brady was present and without her husband's knowledge, I, and the wife, invited them to come to our apartment. Surprisingly she permitted it, "She was more sympathetic to them, than was her husband. When going to our apartment, we had a beautiful prayer meeting, and some sharing time, which further bonded, and knitted our hearts, that much more together.

In short, they were like a breath of fresh air. Our spirits, and hearts, seemed to knit, and bond together, for whatever reason, we didn't know.

And if we ever needed a lift, it was then, for the storm clouds were beginning to gather, again. Shortly after our meeting, they invited the wife, and I, to their house church, in the rural area of Crossville, for a little music. The singing, and rejoicing, we did that night, was above anything that I can remember. At the conclusion of the little music fest, Mrs. Bonnie handed me a check for $50.00, I couldn't believe it, and we didn't even know them.

While we were still at the Living Life, they were asked to minister in song, at the chapel, and it was a sure thing that they always resurrected, some dead and dried bones, and to be sure some eyebrows. If there ever needed to be some resurrection, it was there.

Well by now, Bro. Brady the owner was not happy to find out, that I was now going to the house church that the two families, had established, as opposed to Rev. Wood's church, or to his mission chapel.

Shortly afterwards, as he saw me leaving one evening, for services, he approached me, and asked me, if I was going to church?

I said: "Yes."

He reminded me, of the obligation I had to go to his mission chapel held routinely seven days a week. I reminded him, of the permission he had given me earlier to attend a different church,

He said, that was to be Rev. Woods church only, and no other. And then stated that if I went to the other church that night that I needed to pack my bags now, and leave. And if I didn't, he would do so, and I would find them on the porch, when I came home.

Just another example: of his tyrant, like control, over whom ever.

Quite an ultimatum for which I am not used to, but as of yet, we had not saw the prison gate, for which had always opened prior to our moving.

So we remained at the dead dry services, with much apprehension for the continuation of our stay.

Within a week, as I opened my eyes for the morning, I noticed that the prison gate was present. As the day progressed, it slowly opened, and by 4:00 PM it was totally opened. I know sooner realized that it was totally opened, then I saw two of the directors coming over to our house, and I knew, just as surely as I could, that they was going to tell me to move. They immediately reminded me, again, that the place was a hand's up operation, and not a hand's out operation.

They immediately told me that I needed to go get a job. I said: "Not so" " Bro. Brady told me, I didn't have to get a secular job.

When they couldn't reconcile with me, the fact of a job, they said: "That I should call a number of churches and donate my help to them." They gave me the understanding, that they as directors had as much authority, as Bro. Brady did, and that if I didn't show some progress within the next few days, I would be out. And then one of the directors, a local pawnshop owner, told me to go sweep the front walk off, in front of the chapel.

I told him: "I couldn't do that, because of my back, and shortness of breath, and he encounter with a bunch of muttering, in a low, but half audible voice.

By Friday, we was given a notice, to move the following Wednesday. I asked Bro. Brady the problem, and he said: "That his operation was not geared to house evangelist, and that he would never do so again." I asked him, if that was his final word, and he reiterated his sincere desire, and command, for us to move.

For the last week or so we had no contact, with the ladies, albeit we had the phone numbers. We had come to learn after the fact, that they had been sent as prophets, to minister at the Living Life, and to the owners James & Donna Brady but they would take no heed. As they prepared to leave, The Holy Spirit, prompted them to stay for just one more thing, but didn't elaborate as to what that would be. But like me, they knew from the first time they saw, the wife and I (although not sure within their own hearts and mind) that we were the reason for their call being prolonged, at the Living Life. Mrs. Bonnie often refers to me, as almost, a double take of her father, Jim Bedard, for as she says, along with the rest of her family, that I, look almost like him. By her own admission, the first day they saw the wife and me, in the dining room, they pulled out Jim Bedard picture, for they couldn't believe how much I resembled him.

Well as we stated earlier, we was running out of places to go. We did come to learn that there is another shelter at Cooksville, TN. 35 to 45 miles to the West of Crossville, but that is connected to the one we was in, and by now our welcome at this place was no longer valid.

BUDGET INN

WED 04-28-04 TO TUES. 05-04-04

On that fateful day, we loaded our meager possessions into our Volvo, and shook the dust off of our feet, with little or no remorse, and headed for sight unknown. Having helped out, at the Family Together as alluded to earlier, I was aware of some helps programs, and was able to raise enough money for a week's rent, at the Budget Inn south 127. Surprisingly Budget Inn, would allow their name to be attached to such a rundown filthy place, but never the less, it was a place to hang our hat. When opening the door to the motel room, one could leap onto the bed because of the room being so small. In order to sleep in the room, the wife, had to scrub the walls down, as they were a dark yellow, caused by continuance of cigarette smoke. We stayed in that room one night, and fortunately they gave us a different room for the balance of our stay. It was just nice to be out of the prison environment, at the Living Life. After getting settled into the motel we made contact with the two ladies, and they were anxious, and quick, to come see us. For the balance of our stay, at the Motel, we became acquainted more than ever, and our relationship with them took on a whole new meaning. While together, we had some beautiful prayer times, sharing with each other about our faith walks.

We knew that we had only seven days, to find housing, and we were not sure as to where that might be. The two ladies likewise, were interested as to where we might go, and we all begin to make it a matter of prayer.

One evening towards the end of our prayer, Ms. Bonnie spoke up, and said: "She saw a wheel barrow." We all exclaimed! a wheel barrow! Why on earth would you be seeing a wheel barrow? She said: "I don't know, but I see it very plain and clear."

In the mean time, Sister Bonnie and her husband had been negotiating with an elderly gentleman by the name of John Robb, in the rural area of Crossville. He had a small building, on part of his land that he had previously been using as a church, and they were interested in trying to secure it for their ministry.

On Monday, the two ladies, along with my wife, Ms Judy decided, that they would go talk to him, about the building. Having done so, they begin to tell Mr. Robb of our need for housing.

He told them, that he had a basement apartment, which was vacant at the time, and that he would be interested in renting it out. With that, he gave them the key, and when going downstairs to view the apartment, of all things that could have been in the apt, was a wheel barrow, setting in the middle of the living room. Well, everyone went ecstatic because of the vision, Ms. Bonnie had seen earlier. It seemed to be confirmation from the Holy Spirit that we were to move there.

Earlier, I had always been guided by a prison gate, which would open when time to move, and then close, until the next time to move. It appeared that The Lord was using Ms. Bonnie to help us out, in location of our next place. For what reason, I was not sure. Ms. Bonnie was a prophetess by her own words, and I believe, that The Lord was verifying the validity of her proclamation to me, for where I had come from, even though I was Pentecostal, I had major doubts, about such a calling. In the previous church, that I alluded to earlier, at Pearl City, I had had limited contact, as assistant pastor with a gentleman, by the name of John Nash who claimed to be prophet. The pastor had invited him to the church one night, for a speaking engagement. At that particular time, I didn't know that there was such a calling. I well remember, the many prophecies he gave over the people, at the church, and likewise the ones he gave over the wife, and I, which all proved to be more then true. Now God was allowing me, the privilege of knowing one, and later to work with not only her, as a prophetess, but her husband Rev. George Green as an apostle. My! What a challenge.

By now, it was a known fact to the two ladies, that we had no income, for which to pay rent, or buy food. Also, they were aware of my limitations, on accepting secular employment, and or confessing need to get government help, such as food stamps, for which I would have been entitled too.

Power of God Ministries for which they represented, was just a house church, with no more, then two, to three families, attending, and yet here they were in the process of supporting the wife and I in full.

JOHN ROBB, TUES. 05-04-04 TO: MONDAY 08-23-04

With the above in mind, they made arrangements for us to move in Bro. Robb's apartment, assuming all of the rent, and electric bill.

Following our move, they kept us in a continual supply of groceries.

Likewise they provide us with all of the necessary furniture, that we needed.

The same evening Bro Green went shopping unknown to me, to buy me some new clothes, and shoes.

By now, they had housed us, clothed us, fed us, and provide us some needed furniture, and provided for us, in every way, that there was a need. To God be, the Glory.

In addition, they were able to work out an agreement with the owner for occupation of the church, which provided me a place to preach, for the duration of our stay, with a weekly speaking fee.

My! God is good: He has been more then faithful, in every area of our life.

05-22-04

Our son from Indiana, along with his girlfriend, paid us a visit, concerned that his mom was being held prisoner by me, in this faith walk. Having observed the love that the both of us had for each other, He left fully convinced that everything was ok. The following day, he returned, along with his sister and brother in law, and the grandbabies, still very much disgruntled, that we had not stayed in contact with them. Rumor after rumor had surfaced that I had been holding their mom hostage, as it were, and keeping her from them, but as they found out she was well, in agreement with me. It was just another way for Satan, to attack us.

On one weekend in particular, Ms. Bonnie's sister came from Baltimore on a visit, and while there, Ms. Bonnie asked her to preach. At the end of her sermon, she was calling people up front to prophesy over them, as she did me. Following her prophesy over me, and in the middle of her prophesy over someone else, she turned to me, and said: "Bro. Bill the Lord just told me, to tell you, that the mighty oak has fallen." What a puzzling statement.

That got my attention real quick. Following service, I asked Ms. Bonnie, what she meant by such a statement, and she said "I don't know, go ask her." When doing so, she said, she didn't know. She only did as The Lord had instructed her.

As I begin to search the scriptures, I come to learn, that the oak tree, is recognized as a symbol of strength, and now she had stated that I had fallen. Shortly thereafter, I begin to see a large wood chipper, and a large oak tree was being lifted into the bin of the chipper, by a large crane, and being fed into the chipper. Shortly afterwards, I saw, as it were the Lord Jesus taking the chips out of the chipper bin, and reorganizing them back into a nice quality green tree. While observing this vision The Lord gave the explanation that I would go forth in the residual. Puzzled, I asked The Lord: what that meant, He pointed me to a dictionary, and when I looked it up, I come to find out that residual means the left over part, or the useable part. He explained to me, that I was going to be sent out, in the residual, (the left over, and useable part,) and that He would be the missing part.

One day shortly after moving into the residence, the two ladies paid us a visit, wishing to talk with me about revelation that they had received from The Lord about me. The Lord had given me the last few months Luke 1:76 (a prophetic call) Now they had come down to tell me that The Lord was prompting them, to tell me of the prophetic call. Well, I had asked The Lord for confirmation, and now he was giving it to me, through them. Well the best way that I could describe my feelings at that time was amazement.

Little did I know at the time, that both couples, the original founders of the church, had the same calling on their life as I did: Now then: I was able to join with them, in unity.

Ran Lawnmower up the tree

While at the residence, I assisted Mr. Robb with mowing his yard using his riding lawnmower, and one day, while doing so, I had approached a tree rather fast, as I had often done, but failed to turn it quick enough, consequently running the mower up the tree, and over turned it. As result, I tore out my right shoulder rendering it useless, until having surgery on the rotator cup. I am not sure why this happened, but I feel perhaps God was trying to tell me to stay in the critical vain of thought, for which it would be easy to get out of.

A good part of this faith walk, has been waiting, and concentrating, on God, through prayer, reading, and study of His Word, with praise and worship. I want to say here, that many times, it would have been easier, for me to have went to work, then to set idle especially after having been involved in full time ministry, but again, I believe, it was just part of the test. In actuality when one is staying within that critical vain of thought, he is not setting idle, but is very much within the center of God's will. Since having lost the ministry at Pearl City reference the church, nursing home, and jail, we have preached and ministered very little, compared to the past.

For many months, I believed God would bring me into fulltime ministry, when in fact, we had little, or no ministry.

Again, I allude to my friend, who I mention earlier, Bro RK Storey who spent four years, in a concentration camp, and he stated, that he could do very little ministry, except to memorize Bible Verses. Thanks to The Precious Lord, I now know many verses, by memory. I can say, with deep gratitude in my heart, that I have never regretted this faith walk, and again, I thank God, that He gave the wife, and I, the fortitude and strength to forge ahead, when seemingly all Hell was against us.

One day while sitting in the car, just observing, I looked up, and I saw a mountain lion coming out of the woods towards me. As it begin to cross the road, a speeding car a short distance away, scared it, and it turned around, and ran back into the woods. I always will believe that the Lord was reminding me of the old prophet in the book of 1 Kings 13:24

LION STORY IN BIBLE

By now, our friends begin to feel, that their call to this particular church, was beginning to run out. They along with Bro. Robb had received many revelations, reference the ongoing operation of the church, reference, Power of God Ministries, and in fact, had received ample warnings, from God about the validity of the church, and its continuation, in this stance, but he was determined to have, and to follow his own pernicious ways. A short time later, I begin to see Angels on the front side of his church building holding a sign saying Icabod. 1 Samuel 4:21 meaning the Glory of God has Departed.

A short time later, he gave the church notice, for me to vacate, the apartment, and for them to end, their occupancy of the church, for which they had to return, to their house church, in the rural area of Crossville.

As always, God raised some one up to help us out, and this time was no different. A short while before vacation of these premises, Ms. Bonnie and Ms. Linda had come into fellowship, with another minister, by the name of Bro. Eric Johnson. He presently was trying to establish a Hispanic church, in the area, for the Spanish speaking people, and likewise had a number of rentals in the area. As result, Ms. Bonnie made Bro. Johnson aware of our need for housing.

He like many others did not agree with our faith walk, saying that we had to put legs to our prayers, but despite his denial, he consented, to give us housing because of POWER OF GOD Ministries being involved.

ERIC JOHNSON

08-24-04 to 09-24-04

On that given day, we moved our possessions into one of his apts. On Main St: approximately six buildings to the south of the former Family Together Shelter. Strangely enough, I had made previous contact with Bro. Johnson, while working, and living at The Family Together Shelter, in hopes of finding a building to house the Shelter.

The building, consist of four apartments, for which one could be used as a mission, and the other three apartments for a shelter. Matter of fact; plans were drawn up to that end, but to date, it has not happened.

One of the tenants, by the name of Faez Kingston, in an effort to help the landlord maximize the full rent potential, and in as much as he was only paying a partial rent, because of using his apartment for sleeping purposes only, gave permission to the landlord, for the wife and I to move into his apartment. POWER OF GOD Ministries was charged the balance of the normal rent, and our share of the electric bill,

Having moved our possession into the apartment, we continued our occupancy there for one month. Two problems, surfaced immediately, the first problem was cigarette smoke. As result, I asked Faez, if he could smoke outdoors, for which he consented to do.

Secondly, we continued our anointed prayer meetings at this place, for which Faez was not used too, consequently he became disgruntled, and decided that it would be better for him to move elsewhere, so with that in mind he moved. After his move, that left the landlord short of the needed income, for that apartment, and in as much as the church was unable to take on the full load of the apartment rent, along with the electric bill, they were unable to continue to support our occupancy there.

By the end of the month, it became very clear, that time had run out, for this place. By this time POWER OF GOD Ministries, had returned to their house church.

We still had no income, beyond what we received from our speaking activities through the church.

As stated earlier, The church was well aware of our limitations reference accepting secular employment, and or confessing need, to get government help, such as food stamps, etc., for which I would have been entitled too. They seemed to be at a cross road, as to whether they would continue to pay our rent, and or buy our food.

By Ms. Connie's own words, they had been closely discerning, or scrutinizing, us, and watching every move we made. They could not understand why, I could not hold secular employment, and or confess need, such as getting food stamps, etc. It didn't make any sense to them, in as much as Ms. Connie's husband held secular employment full time, even though he was sick much of the time, and Ms. Linda's husband was recuperating, from a severe injury, while on his former job. To add injury to insult, she continually referred to Paul's tent making job, in order that he might not be a burden see Acts 18:3, and could see no wrong, or harm, in me seeking secular employment.

I reiterated the command that I had received from The Lord, reference secular employment, and, or confessing need, and stood firm on my conviction.

In rebuttal to Ms. Connie, I posed the question, reference confessing need, What would you have said, if I had approached any one of you, and ask you to help me out, because I just didn't feel it right to hold secular employment. Would you have done so? I stated: "You would have told me to get up off of my lazy behind, and go to work, and then I wouldn't have any need."

As I reminded them, I did not ask, or tell any one of them to support us. It was The Lord's doing only: not mine. Ref. Dan: 4:35

They could not argue with that statement, for I had not said one word to them about supporting us. I continued my discussion reference confessing need, and told of the book True Discipleship by William Mac Donald. See the section of book at end of book.

Well, in the back of their minds I could see that they had major doubts, about these two commands, but being the great examples they are for The Lord: Bro. Green made the comment, that as long as he had a roof over his head, they would not allow us, to go homeless, and all agreed.

Shortly thereafter, an old friend, of theirs, The Rev. Conrad Welch, a prophet, from Baltimore came to visit, The Greens and the Cook's, and from the comments that were made, he assured them, that such a call that I had received, was legitimate, for he confirmed the fact, that he had not held any secular employment for many years, for which he took a lot of criticism for.

That seemed to put a stop to the questioning for the time being about my work ethic.

The two couples, as part of their faith walk, had been sharing a small three bedroom house having only one bath. The house is located, rural Crossville, TN. The house was adequate for their needs, but when family, or visitors came, it quickly became a severe burden, especially with the one bathroom. Ms. Connie told of times, when she had to literally schedule baths around the clock, to accommodate, all concerned. Not a very pleasant experience. Fortunately, the landlord realizing the problems, offered to move his 27 ft travel trailer on the premises to help relieve the crowded living quarters. However, they still had to rely on the one and only bathroom. At least they had some extra beds.

By now late fall and winter was upon us, and as result of the visitations slowing down, the trailer was not being used, much,

With that in mind, and in as much as they didn't want to see the wife, and I, back on the street, they decided, with their Landlord's permission, to let us live in the trailer. So by their request, we moved our possession into the small travel trailer.

09-24-04 to 04-08-05 THE GREEN PREMISES RURAL CROSSVILLE

Well for the next several months, the small travel trailer became our home. It set within 50ft of our friend's house. It had no utilities, beyond an extension cord, for limited electrical use, and a garden hose for which we used till winter came. There was no sewage connection, and so the wife, and I, was forced to use there already over crowed bath facilities. Likewise, we ate all of our meals at their house, because of limited cooking facilities. Not many individuals would go to this length, to keep a couple from being homeless, but this was their intent, and their call from The Lord.

Likewise, it gave us all, more of a chance to become better acquainted with each other. We had many meaningful times together, in our communion with The Lord Jesus, as well as our daily prayer times, and other daily activities. The Lord seemingly, knit our hearts together, as he did Jonathan, and David's heart 1 Samuel 18:1. We continued our church services, at the house church, and from time to time we would all go to another church for visitation, and that was the case November 5 while we was visiting a church near the town of Crab Orchard, on a Tuesday evening. The small church was having a revival of sorts, by evangelist Dennis and Eureka Daniels Moody, AL. Following service, they begin to call various ones to the front for prophecies. At the tail end of the service, they called me to the front, and gave me some of the most unusual prophecies, I ever heard, certainly encouraging to say the least. I was prophesied over by three different individuals, which all seemed to line up with what The Lord had already given me. At the end of the service, the small church served refreshment, in a time of fellowship. It was during that fellowship, that I begin to feel again, that horrible pain within my heart. The same thing that I had experienced while at The Family Together Shelter might near a year before. Following some prayer being offered on my behalf, we cut short our visit and returned home. The pain finally subsided within two to three hours, and we forgot about it. The following night, we all returned to the small church for another service, and following church, as we was setting around talking to each other the pain became more severe than ever, in my heart. Again after more prayer, we returned home but unlike before, the pain did not stop. I was later rushed to the hospital for a number of physical test, Unawares, that I had already left for the hospital, Bro. Green came out of his bedroom to tell me about a stint that he saw them putting in my heart.

Having found out that I had already left for the hospital he told Ms. Connie. Knowing that I did not like to discuss physical ailments etc. she then waited to see what the test results were.

The following day, following the test, the hospital physicians notified the wife, and I, that I had two blockages, and wanted to transfer me to Cookeville TN. hospital for surgery. In the back of my mind, I rejected any thought of such surgery, especially open heart surgery, for I always felt, that I would be the last one, to have such a thing happened to me. Within the same time frame, Ms. Connie arrived on the scene, to inform the wife, and I, of the stint Bro. Green had seen, in a vision. At about the same time, a peace came over me that everything would be alright.

Without the word from The Apostle Bro. Green I no doubt, would have declined the surgery, but The Lord knew the exact timing for Ms. Connie to show up, and I, consented to have a stint put in, and with that they sent me to Cookesville, TN. for the surgery. Because of some other lingering surgeries, they continued to keep me in ICU over the weekend, and on Monday morning, they transferred me, to the operating room. I shall never forget, that as I was lying, there, being prepared for that surgery, The Lord Jesus, was there, looking over the entire situation. Yea though I walk thru the valley of the shadow of death I will fear, no evil. See Psalms 23 Some say, you can't see Jesus like that, but I want to reiterate in the strongest possible way, that I know how, that ever since, I have entered into the last part of this faith walk, He, The Lord Jesus, has always been bigger than life itself, and by my side 24/7, Acts 2:25 & 26 and that day was no exception. Well we didn't know where this was leading too, but I knew that God was in control. When we came out of the hospital we had near $70,000.00 in medical bills, but then The Lord took care of them too by allowing us to get Tenn. Care, which not only paid for our surgery, it provided the necessary medicine, at a average cost of $500.00 per month, over the next several months. At a later date because of having Tenn. Care, I was able to have my rotator cup, repaired in my arm.

Well as I stated, timing was very critical for this problem, for had it happened before we met our Divine Connection, the wife would have been as it were by herself, so far as any earthly friends. But our friends, were there to stand by her side, even though, her life seemed to be falling apart before her very eyes. They continually offered her, their continual support through the whole ordeal. Following my surgery, and short recovering, I continued to preach, at the house church, and continued my daily activity the best I could, under the conditions, although severely limited by doctor's orders.

By the time that all of this was over, The Thanksgiving and Christmas Season was upon us. Throughout the whole holiday season, it was good to be with some friends that we could trust. Brother Robert, and Ms. Linda aware that we had been separated for over a year from our grandbabies, living in the Pearl County area, felt to give us $50.00, and the use of their van, to buy some Christmas for them, and then to take the gifts to them. God's love and generosity seemed to show thru both couples, in even a greater way, then what we had known before.

Likewise the wife, and I, received many gifts, from both couples. This Christmas season, is one that the wife, and I, will always remember.

As we begin to move into the New Year, I begin to feel a tug on my heart to apply for food stamps. I, at first rejected this thought, but The Lord reminded me, that I could not work, even if I wanted too, because of the recent heart surgery. He also showed me, that I had done all to stand and now it was his turn to provide for me through this method. See Ephesians 6:12-15

Within just a short time, Bro. Green made a similar comment, and within a day or so Ms. Linda unawares of my message from The Lord, advised the same, and likewise Bro. Green's admonition, suggested, that I, in as much as I couldn't work, ought to apply for food stamps. Their son Jonathan made the argument that Joseph's brother, having run out of substance, in their land came for help in Egypt. Genesis 40-50, I shared all of this information with Ms. Connie, and likewise she felt very much at peace with me getting food stamps.

They all were well aware, that I had done all I could, to stand, and now they were all in agreement with me, for signing up for food stamps.

By the wife, and I, getting food stamps, something that I had never done before, it relieved them of the burden of our support, so far as food.

But that did not help the high dollar heating bills, for the trailer.

For by now, we was in the main part of winter, and in as much as the travel trailer was not a four seasoned unit, we were going through propane gas, like water, causing a lot of concern on their part, because of their low income. Even though they had a church in the house, they still were receiving very little in tithes, and offerings. Much prayer went up by all concerned, and to make matter worse, the owner, by now was, wanting, his trailer back, for a early spring camping trip. Knowing how we felt, about moving into their house, they begin to tell us the choices we had, for which we already knew, which did not look good.

By now, March was upon us, and Bro. Green began to feel a tug on his heart, to have me apply for Government Housing. I had already done that while at the Living Life, and I knew what the outcome would be. I informed him of the fact, that I was not eligible for government housing because of me owing a bill to the Pearl County Housing Authority, by my previous tenure mentioned earlier.

However, he had contact, with a man in Rhea County, who was personally acquainted with the Head Man, over the Housing Authority in the County of our residence, and insisted that Ms. Connie, and I, would have a talk with him. Upon doing so, we found that he was less then sympathetic to our need, but did give us the criteria for my occupancy within the housing unit. That being that the $695.00 that we owed, Pearl County Housing, would have to be paid. Ms. Connie asked if it could be paid in installments, or if it had to be paid in full. He indicated that Pearl County Housing would have to make that decision.

The fact, that I was disabled, as result of my heart and arm, and the fact that we were living in what they call sub-standard housing put me at the top of the list, but he still gave little hope because of the low vacancy rate.

Following contact with him, we made contact with the Pearl County Housing Authority, and they stated, that if the church would guarantee payment, that we would be permitted to pay $100.00 per month, and would give us a release for Cumberland County Housing to rent to us.

When disclosing this information to Cumberland County Housing, they immediately sent an inspector out to the premise, to see if in fact we were living in substandard house. Within three days of their visit we received a call from Housing saying that they had a handicap unit for us, in the small community of Pleasant Hill, rural Crossville.

At this time, the Church entered into agreement, with Pearl County Housing Authority, to pay $100.00 per month, and then took the agreement and the release to Crossville Housing, and they immediately rented us an apartment.

Just another example, of God's Love showing through. It brought to remembrance, of how Paul paid a debt for Oneimus in the 1 John

The fact, that Pleasant Hill is near twenty miles to the west of Crossville, presented some problems, because of no immediate transportation, and the high gas, but we knew that God was in control.

04-08-05 PLEASANT HILL CLEARVIEW LN. APT 1.
Well unlike before, I was severely limited, by the amount of moving, that I could do, but God provided and made the way.

Again God made all of the provision necessary, for our independent occupancy at this location. He even provided the wife, with a washer, and lawn mower, in as much as we were responsible for keeping our yard mowed.

From time to time, the two couples joined us, in having church at our residence as opposed to their house in rural Crossville, because of high fuel prices.

09-23-04 – 09-17-06 Just shortly before moving to the Green's residence our 84 Volvo (see remarks about this car) bit the dust rendering it useless. That left us without any wheels. Much prayer was made reference a car, in as much as it put a heavy burden on The Green family & The Cook Family

For nearly two years both families supported us in every need we had, including full transportation etc. Because of having no wheels both families drove hundreds of miles, on our behalf. To God:, BE THE GLORY.

Well again God is alive, and well on planet earth. We continued to stand on Micah 7:7 and sure enough on

09-2005 The Lord put it upon the heart of a beautiful Jewish couple, a miracle all of its own, in the Crossville area to give us a 95 Buick with only 38500 miles on it, with no debt or car payment. God has been faithful in every way.

Beginning 01-2006 I was blessed with receiving retirement income from social security, in 01-2007 the wife begin to receive retirement funding from social security.

And in 05-07 the Lord allowed us to move into a beautiful two bedroom house free from any cigarette smoke.

The thing that thrills my soul, Over and over, as of the time of this writing is, that God has been very faithful, in his commitment to me, reference secular employment.

He asked me to trust Him for fulltime ministry, with no secular employment, and likewise I took Him at His Word. To recap I retired from the business world 10-31-96, and lived on my liquidated investments, through Mid 98, and from that time forward, we have not held any secular employment, beyond what was mentioned in the forepart of this book. The wife, and I, walked by faith only. Only God could have done that.

84 VOLVO, THE SCREAMING DEMON (a very apt description)

The car that we received from the lady at the housing authority was a 84 Volvo. It was as one minister put it a car that you wanted to park four to five blocks from where you were attending church, hoping that no one would even connect you with the car.

The muffler and tailpipe had separated, causing them to hang lower than usual. We tried to keep them wired in place, but that too became impossible to deal with.

One would have no trouble locating us, as we left a blue trail of smoke wherever we went, not to mention the fact that our clothes always smelled of burnt oil fumes, which continually saturated the car. Much of that was contributed to the fact that only one of the four electric windows worked, and one that had to be propped up, which rob us of the ability to keep fresh air in the car at all times. Going to the Green's house one day unannounced and them not being familiar with our car, said it sounded like Jed Clampit's, car well known from The Beverly Hillibillies.

The second problem that we encounter with the car was the chimer that alerts one to the fact that the keys are still in the ignition. For some reason the thing got a short in it, and it continually chimed, ding, ding, ding one hundred percent of the time. By the time that you had been in the car for any length of time, you were ready to go bonkers or crazy from the crazy chining. We knew that it was somewhere under the dash but trying to locate it was maddening, for the sound echoed from one side to the other when trying to locate it by ear. I inquired of the Volvo dealership of the problem and the estimated cost for having it removed, was well in the excess of $100.00, consequently making it impossible for me to do anything about it. Having endured it for a few weeks, we came to the realization that we could no longer endure the problem. One day while still at the apartment complex, I came across two men working on their car, and approached them about taking the chimer out. Loving to work on cars and thinking that it would be a 15 minute picnic, they accepted the challenge. Little did they know that they would have to dismantle most of the dash to get to it. When finding it they found that the speaker on the chimer was turned toward the firewall under the dash. They both worked feverously on it for at least four hours. We named it the screaming demon, and believe, me, it was just that a screaming demon.

It was a prime suspect for a car of this nature to be stopped by the police, if for nothing more than to be unsafe, but fortunately even though we had the car might near two years, not one time did we get stopped, even though we passed many police units.

The car had a sun roof, which was off track, and would not close properly. We rarely drove the car when it was raining, but one time while en route to Plainview TN. approximately 100 miles to where we had accepted housing with a divine assignment, every time we turned a corner or went around a curve one of us would get wet. Alluded to earlier the electric window, on the driver's side was broke, and would continually fall down, inside the door, with no way to properly secure it. The defrosters was not adequately working, and to make matters worse the windshield wiper on the driver's side, was stripped out at its connection point and would only work when it wanted, which didn't seem to be that day. Fortunately we had an umbrella, for which we put up in the car, to help shield us from rain, but even with that we both were soaked to the gills, along with everything we had in the car, blankets, clothing, and what baggage we couldn't get in the trunk.

But we continued toward our destination, even though it seemed as all the powers of hell was against us.

After one of the most frustrating trips of our life we were finally able to meet our connection, as we agreed.

Towards the last of our ownership of the screaming demon, and of all times in the winter, the driver's side door window fell down inside the door, and when trying to retrieve it, it shattered. With little heat, and the fan not working, one made sure that he was dressed adequately when driving.

On one given occasion, having gone, to the store, I shut the engine off, and retrieved the key from the ignition, and immediately the end of the key drop off, and fell to the floor. Had God not been looking out for us, we would have been without transportation inasmuch as we would have needed a locksmith to retrieve the broken key.

Over and over as alluded to in various stories throughout the book we was required to run gasless, time and time again, until we became comfortable with doing so. Many times I marveled how that could be, especially with a fuel injection engine, for cars are not made to run gasless, but God is alive and well on planet earth, and all things are possible through Him. It received its justified end at the scrap yard.

True Discipleship Defined

To walk by sight means to have visable means of support, to have adequate reserves, for the future, to employ human cleverness, insuring against unseen risk. The walk of faith is the very opposite, it is a moment, by moment reliance on God alone. It is a perpetual crisis of dependence on The Lord. The flesh shrinks from a position of complete dependence on an unseen God. It seeks to provide a cushion against possible losses. If it cannot see where it is going, it is apt to suffer complete nervous collapse. But faith steps forward, in obedience to The Word of God, rises above circumstances, and trusts The Lord, for the supply of all needs. Any disciple, who determines to walk by faith, can be sure that his faith will be tested. Sooner or later, he will be brought to the end of his human resources. In his extremity, he will be tempted to appeal to his fellow men. If he really is trusting the Lord, he will look to God alone.

To make known his wants directly, or indirectly, to a human being, is departure from the life of faith, and a positive dishonor to God. It is actually betraying Him. It is tantamount, to say, that God has failed me, and that I must look to my fellow man for help. It is forsaking the living fountain, and turning to a broken cistern. It is placing the creature, between my soul, and God, thus robbing my soul of rich blessings, and The God of Glory due Him.

Written by William Mac Donald, and published by Walterick Publishers Kansas City, Kansas I received this book, at ordination time (see quote p. 39-40) Used by permission Gospel Folio Press

This book reveals how human beings can be here on Earth.

Jesus is Real Faith is real walk hand in hand every day with Jesus

Faith will always win Melinda Elmore

also available from publishamerica

HEARTS ON THE MEND
by Floriana Hall

It is a known fact that heart disease is the number one killer of women. Understanding that, Floriana Hall feels that she is fortunate to be alive today since she had no apparent symptoms. A chance remark to her family physician led to four different tests before it was found out her main artery was 100 percent blocked, two others ninety-five percent, and one ninety percent. She knew about her genetic factor, but was told that her heart was fine at every doctor's visit.

Floriana experienced a quadruple heart bypass on September 4, 2003. She felt compelled to write her bizarre story to help mankind.

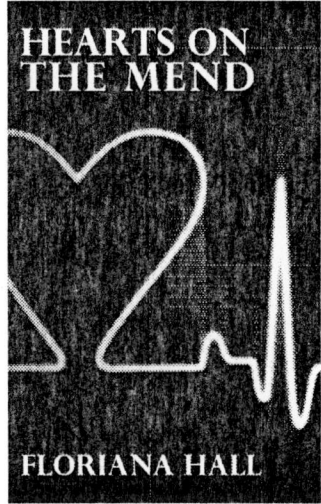

HEARTS ON THE MEND

FLORIANA HALL

Paperback, 78 pages
6" x 9"
ISBN 1-4241-2038-1

About the author:

Floriana Hall, born in Pittsburgh, Pa., on October 2, 1927, is a Distinguished Alumna of Cuyahoga Falls High School, class of 1945. She attended Akron University. She and her husband have been married 60 years, have five children, nine grandchildren and two great-grandchildren. She is a member of St. Martha's church in Akron, Ohio. Floriana has written twelve books, nonfiction and poetry. She is the founder and coordinator of *The Poet's Nook*, a group of local poets who meet monthly at Cuyahoga Falls Library.

available to all bookstores nationwide.
www.publishamerica.com

INSIDE PASSAGE
by Eunice Loecher

Michelle Lawson wins the trip of a lifetime on an Alaskan inside passage cruise. Disaster strikes in Skagway when a tour bus breaks down, leaving Michelle stranded. While struggling with the decision of how to rejoin her ship, Michelle learns Todd Harper has been released from prison. He is a violent stalker who terrorized Michelle the previous year. Returning home to Erie, Pennsylvania, is no longer a safe option.

After finding a job and a place to live for the summer, Michelle believes she's safe. When a newspaper story reveals her location, Todd Harper comes to finish what he started in Erie.

God teaches Michelle to trust and depend on others. Through it all she discovers acceptance, community and the future God has planned for her.

Paperback, 171 pages
5.5" x 8.5"
ISBN 1-60563-732-7

About the author:

Eunice Loecher is an award-winning author of numerous devotionals, essays, and poems. Her novel, *Living Water*, is available through PublishAmerica. You may contact Eunice at crafty2@newnorth.net or visit her website: www.euniceloecher.com.

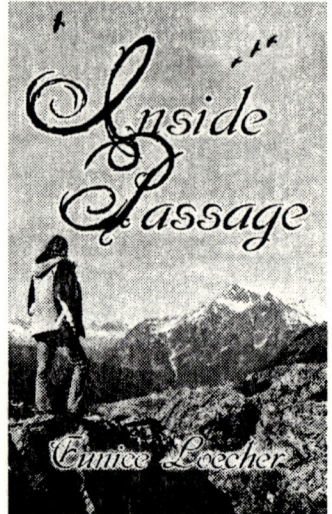

UNICORNS DON'T WEAR SHOES
by Helen M. Hogan

When Wes Wilson discovers a body in the barn where he boards his Quarter horse, he faces unexpected accusation from the chief deputy. Wes postpones his dreams—ofcompeting with his stallion in cutting horse shows and of dating Cathy McLeod. He helps rescue Mrs. Magers' lost pony from the slaughterhouse. Young Susan screams in horror as foreman Sutherland kills the stable cat's kittens, so Wilson wades in. As principal, he hopes to expand his high school's programs against opposition from his vin-dictive superintendent. With his teacher accused of kid-napping, Wes figures out the hiding place. Meanwhile, he learns the murder victim is not Mexican but Syrian and in the U.S. with two others on the Homeland Security watch list. The terrorists move in for an explosive ending.

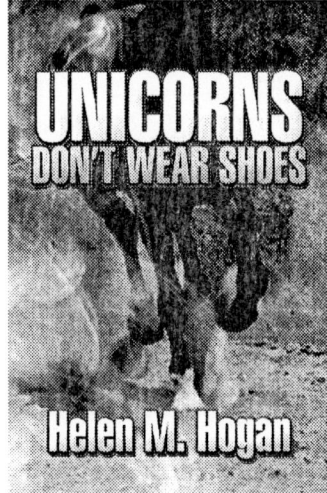

Paperback, 413 pages
6" x 9"
ISBN 1-60441-107-4

About the author:

Retired from teaching college English, Helen judges several horse breeds. She loves traveling with her husband of thirty-eight years, Berry Hogan. The couple enjoy sitting in the backyard swing with a glass of wine and playing with their dogs. Helen M. Hogan's published mysteries include Warning Shot and Driven to Win.

DRAWING CONSTELLATIONS
by Jim Hunter

Galen McNeil always considered himself immune to superstitions…except for this Friday the 13th. One year ago exactly, his girlfriend broke up with him because she claimed God told her to, and Galen can't help but reminisce. His reflections are compounded when an evangelist reads Galen the same passage from the Bible that his ex quoted a year ago that day! The coincidences are almost too much for him when the conversation is interrupted by a beautiful woman who vies for Galen's attention. Stunned by the conflation of past and present, Galen is unable to act and the woman leaves without giving her name or number. For the next week Galen puts up signs in the middle of the park, entreating the woman's return as he tries desperately to regain what was lost and answer tough questions about his life and his place in the world.

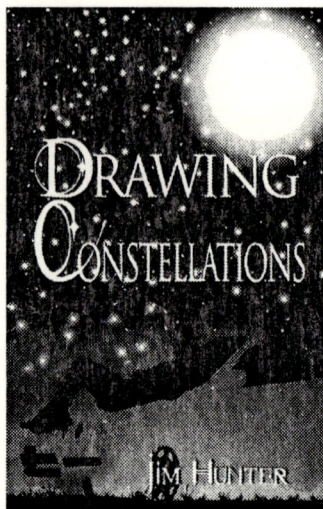

Paperback, 151 pages
5.5" x 8.5"
ISBN 1-4241-7380-9

Filled with fully fleshed characters, staccato, realistic dialogue, an off-beat wit, and a philosophical subtext as poignant as it is heartfelt, *Drawing Constellations* presents a gripping cross-section of our culture and our changing time.

About the author:

Jim Hunter was educated at Miami University, Ohio. He currently lives with his family in Oberlin, Ohio. *Drawing Constellations* is his first novel.